Slowing Down in a Speedstressed World

Practical Skills & Kindly Advice

Marian Read Place, LCSW

Composed Life Press
Durham, North Carolina

www.slowlutions.com
marian@slowlutions.com

Marian Read Place

Composed Life Press
P.O. Box 1223
Durham, N.C. 27702-1223
www.slowlutions.com
marian@slowlutions.com

Artwork and book design by:
Claudia Fulshaw Design
Durham, N.C.
cfdesign19@aol.com

ISBN: 978-0-615-89303-7

My heartfelt thanks to

the many individuals
who generously shared their thoughts and wisdom with me,

and to

all those who offered encouragement as I created this book.

This book is dedicated to

you –

and to everyone

who longs to live a little more slowly each day.

Into the Garden

A summer's evening in the garden: the earth is furrowed and still warm. Windows glow in the house as a screen door opens and Sylvia, a young girl, hops down the step and skips to the garden. Melany follows her daughter, who stops to lean over a plant, her fingers hunting for the smooth round of a cherry tomato. Melany's fingers find one too, in this garden she has tended while Sylvia pulled weeds and skipped about. Each night now they come out and, as the sweet, seedy orbs burst in their mouths, they look at the ivory moon hanging in the night sky. These moments sow memories that take root for later years, sweet as the earthly red jewels mother and daughter have grown together.

It is for "moon and tomato" moments such as these that we slow down.

Contents

Into the Garden, Into this Book

"Be brave enough to love your life. It's your life."

~ April Yvonne Garrett

When Melany Coopmans steps out into a summer evening with her young daughter Sylvia, only the simplest effort is usually required: a turn of her body toward the back door, a slight push on the screen, and the step or two out toward the garden. For the *speedstressed*, though – the many people who regularly move through their days more quickly than they would like in order to lessen their to-dos, as well as their anxiety about them - entering into even a momentary "garden" of calm and balance isn't easy at all.

Had Melany not long followed through with her daily intention to enjoy slow time, taking a break would be difficult for her, too. The temptation to stay focused on tasks might tug harder than her desire for ease and for time with her daughter. Melany might give in to her mind's murmurings of "There's just not enough time" and "I've too much to do" and, as a result, frequently tell Sylvia to go out to the garden by herself.

Were she to do so, their moments savoring tomatoes under the moon would become nothing more than possibilities dissolving into the dark. And, at some future point, Melany

1

might look back to discover she had unintentionally created a life she didn't want: One in which calm, time with loved ones, and beauty's many forms and expressions - to name only a few of the wonders afforded by a slower pace - had faded into the background.

Happily, Melany regularly crosses the distance between acknowledging her anxiety about to-dos and acting on her belief that "slowing down is very important to allow restoration and rejuvenation." As this introduction will outline, and this book will demonstrate, you can too.

Speedstress

The experience of anxiously moving at a pace faster than you would like in order to:

- complete tasks and obligations

and, as a result,

- lessen your anxiety about having those tasks.

Speedstress may be an intermittent experience – or it may become habitual. In the end, it often increases anxiety and costs us time.

Located beneath Madison Square Garden's sports and entertainment extravaganzas, New York's Pennsylvania Station offers its own kind variety show. Trains squeal into the station like grimy metal curtains, severing the view from one side of tracks to the other. Beneath the ever-changing schedule boards and the din of the P.A. system, several hundred thousand passengers dash to their appointed tracks each day.

Penn Station provides an exaggerated representation of many people's hectic, stress-inducing daily pace. In an age of ceaseless incoming information and demands, of lean staffing and veneration of speed, a hasty pace is viewed as the solution for not only "too much to do in too little time," but also for the anxiety we have about that all-too-common dilemma.

If your transit through your to-dos often feels both faster and more anxious than you would like, you are speedstressed. This book's mission is to, small step by small step, help you achieve a more sustainable balance between hurry and slowness, and stress and ease – a balance that, while imperfect and ever-changing, feels more right than living in a state of anxious hurry.

After reading these pages, you will have skills you can call upon to relieve the tension and tiredness that are central to people's experience of speedstress. And, even better: you'll believe that slowing down on a regular basis is not only a right of yours, it's also a benefit to your loved ones and to the work or projects you undertake.

While it will come as little surprise that those who work full-time can easily develop a pace that feels over-hasty, it's also true that the retired and unemployed have no guarantee of immunity from the *too much-too little dilemmas* we'll explore that incite us to hurrying. I say this because speedstress – which often becomes a habitual pattern – originates far less from our multitude of tasks than it does from the way in which we work with our anxiety about them.

Slowlutions®

Any intentional actions (or non-actions) you take in order to:

- *slow your pace,*

- *shift your attention* away from stressors,

  or

- *attend to a need or desire* you've identified as a result of slowing down.

Unlike many books on slowing down, we'll explore how a hasty pace has, in part, been an escape from that anxiety. We'll look at how to work effectively with anxiety – both that sparked by all you have to do and that which often arises as people begin to slow down.

3

These pages are enriched by the wisdom and stories of interviewees and of anonymous respondents to a pace-of-life survey I sent across the country. They characterize life at a near-unrelenting fast pace with terms such as "horrendous ... tremendous impact ... erosion." Kept up too long, *speed*stress can result in poor health, strained relationships and, ironically, errors that cost more time than one's haste ever could have saved. As illustration of that last point, we'll dip back a few years, down into the crowd of travelers at Penn Station. There, a friend of mine, an executive, was eager to return home to her family in Maryland after meetings in her branch office in New York.

My friend was simultaneously navigating the crowd, working her BlackBerry, and listening for the announcement of her train. Hearing notification of a departure, she rushed to the track "instead of taking an extra ten seconds to check the [schedule] board." Minutes later, as the train began gliding from the station, my friend realized she was bound for Boston.

There is a lesson here which I encourage you to take to heart: If ten seconds *not* taken has the power to disrupt one's plans and equanimity, then that interval *taken* has the power to cultivate the opposite effect. Using slowlutions® regularly and briefly as part of a practice called *i slow* will help you reshape not only your pace, but your stress level and sense of personal control.

Slowlution® is a funny word, but it's one with a purpose. The tension and fatigue, the driven-ness of speedstress can cause humor and playfulness to seem frivolous or, even, wrong; silliness can seem to invite a relaxation we feel we can ill afford. Consequently, I coined slowlution® to inject a bit of whimsy where it is badly needed - and to represent slowing down as the solution it is for speedstress. With time and practice, *"What's my slowlution®?"* will prove a helpful trigger for new and empowering choices.

I encourage you to think of each slowlution® you put into practice as a seed from which you are growing a new pace of life. Seed by seed, you *will* do so. But, be realistic: As with gardening, slowing down is not without challenges. Your accustomed pace will, no less than a weed, spring up again and again. Staying on the run can be "almost like a magnet," says novelist and single parent Zelda Lockhart. "I sometimes feel pulled toward all of the frenzy ... It becomes too easy then to continue to stay in that energy when it's not necessary anymore."

So, as you begin slowing down, expect that you'll forget to do so. Expect, too, that anxiety about your demands, or thoughts about the impossibility of slowing down, will hijack your pace. Certainly, our speedstressed culture will pull you away from change.

That's o.k.; in fact, it's all part of the process. Like a neglected garden patch, any lapse in slowing down needs little for its revival other than your decision to once again turn your attention to it. I'll encourage you throughout these pages to respond to your imperfect efforts with kindness and persistence.

As you become increasingly skilled at rebalancing your pace and stress level, you'll notice some liberating shifts. The attention you bring to work or other projects will improve, as will your outlook. You'll experience not only greater calm, but a reconnection with yourself and others. And, circumstances that you once thought of as hindrances to task completion – for example, a wait on line or a long bus ride home – you'll come to consider a welcome patch of spare time in which to cultivate calm or enjoyment.

Attorney Janna Greeley's* experience in the Times Square subway station provides hopeful proof of this. Located just

* Name altered at interviewee's request. In total, four interviewees, most of whom you'll meet early on in these pages, requested this. Three of them did so out of fear that talking about slowing down would harm their professional lives - a telling commentary on our speedstressed culture.

fifteen blocks north of Penn Station, Times Square's convergence of subway lines can easily sweep travelers along in its speed-stressed energy. As Janna recalls, "Every cell in your body is on the highest speed. You're wrapped up in this frenzy of people zooming."

Many people might dispute the possibility of slowing down in such a speedstressed environment. However, Janna found it was entirely possible – even as the crowd of travelers gripping sharp-edged briefcases pressed against her. "The best way to cope with being there is to walk really slowly," Janna says. "Slowing yourself in a fast-paced environment is very powerful. Running like a crazy person is no guarantee you're going to get where you want to go."

Imagine the sense of control Janna felt as she opted to slow down as scores of people rushed by her. Now, contrast that feeling with the resignation I heard one day in the voice of a customer exiting a bookshop. "Sorry to be in such a rush," the woman called out, "it's the story of our lives."

It doesn't have to be. If hurry has crowded out the life-story you yearn to create, I encourage you to refocus on what's real and true: That you were not born to live like a commuter trying to cover the distance to her track in less than half the time needed. You were born for balance: For the dash, yes, that the gardener sometimes makes to get seeds in the ground, but also for the slow joy of noticing sprouting seedlings, for the careful tending of delicate roots.

I hope this book will help you rededicate to cultivating what is yours only once: *This* life under this sky, with those you love now; the life that's *yours* – not your boss's or anyone else's.

What's my slowlution®? ... for practice or pondering.

≋ Make this book your own: Keep it visible and handy; write in it. Set your intention to pick up these pages regularly; when you do, count reading and pondering even a single paragraph as a success. I hope you'll treat the thoughts and practices in these pages as gifts that you are kindly offering yourself at the pace that works for you.

≋ Begin familiarizing yourself with the steps of *i slow,* the slowlution with which you'll initially seed your new pace. (Be sure to read Chapters 11-14 before using *i slow.*)

	Your seed: i slow	
i	**intentionally**	and regularly (4 times/day):
s	**say**	"I slow" as you take a slow, deep breath
	stop or **slow**	your *pace*
	scan	your *energy level & tension*
l	**listen**	for the answer to *What's my slowlution?*
o	**opt**	to enter into your slowlution, for 30 seconds or more, with as much <u>focus</u> as is safely possible.
w	**watch**	actively for reward(s).

Crowded out
of the Garden

The Speedstressed
Story of Life

Chapter 1

All Roads Lead to One: Speedstress' Three Dilemmas

One: *Too much to do in too little time*
Two: *Too much time with too little to do*
Three: *Too much expense for too little income*

~ Three Dilemmas

San Francisco's dawn fog often makes a cocoon around Dave Banner's* condo building. Given a few hours, the sun burns the thick mist away to reveal the charm of pastel homes and green succulents set along winding streets. On most weekday mornings, Dave outpaces the sun in achieving a slow burn. With words that are tense and hurried, the purchasing executive tells the story of his speedstressed life, one in which he is geared up from the moment he rises:

"The alarm goes off in the morning and so you get up to start your day and you make breakfast, you make coffee, you get your clothes ready, you make your lunch, you get dressed, and head off to work. From the minute that you get up you're receiving data, you're thinking about your emails, you're thinking about your projects, you're thinking about is the bus going to be late, so you're already stressed before you even leave the house.

Then you get to work and then you deal with all the ins and outs of whatever job you're in. You do that all day, then you stop work, you deal with the commute home, then you eat dinner, take some time for yourself, hopefully. You go to bed, and you do this five days a week, six days a week. When is there time for friends? When is there time for yourself? When do you relax? When are you allowed to slow down and not check email?"

Dave is anxious, rushed, and focused on the tasks ahead. In short, he is speedstressed. Based on his comments, I'd guess that Dave would describe himself as *extremely* stressed. If so, he's not alone. A 2012 American Psychological Association (APA) survey on stress reports that nearly a quarter of adults put themselves in that category, while 44 percent report that their stress has increased over the past five years. Dave – and, perhaps, you – might agree with another finding from that survey: lack of time is viewed as a major barrier to making changes that would lessen one's stress.

Is this the story of your life?

If you, like Dave, move anxiously through more days than *you* like at a pace faster than *you* feel comfortable with, you are speedstressed. (Please take care not to belittle or deny your speedstress by comparing yourself others. If you feel hurried and stressed, you are, even if the person next to you isn't.) You may walk, drive, eat, talk, or, as one person told me, "sleep," faster than feels right for you. Often, your pace and focus on task completion result in a lack of clear awareness of your bodily and emotional experiences, as well as of the activity around you. When fatigue, hunger, or desires do become apparent, speed-stress may cause you to ignore them in favor of pushing through your list.

When hurried *doing* becomes too predominant, our per-sonal reality – our meaning in life, as well as our in-the-body experience – can be trampled flat as grasses under horses' hooves. Our existence begins to resonate with a multitude of unintended denials: of our own needs and dreams; of the costs of staying on the run; of the nurture we and loved ones require. Deep within, sadness permeates because this is not the way we truly want to live. Even so, we feel caught in our *too much–too little dilemma.*

Dave falls into the speedstress-inducing dilemma, "too much to do in too little time." This dilemma represents the primary mindset and circumstances that underlie living in a tense rush. However, we'll also explore two additional dilemmas that act much like a starter's gun at a race, causing people to accelerate into the first, or primary, dilemma. The three are:

Too Much-Too Little Dilemmas

	Demand		Resource
#1	Too much to do	*in*	too little time
	Most affected:		*employed; parents*
#2	Too much time	*with*	too little to do
	Most affected:		*retirees/job-seekers*
#3	Too much expense	*for*	too little income
	Most affected:		*job-seekers/retirees/in-debt*

Which *too much–too little* is driving your tension and fast pace? If you don't see one here that applies to you, ask yourself what demand is causing you to live - or eat or shop or drive - too fast because you perceive its related resources to be inadequate?

However you answer that question, any speedstress-inducing dilemma is usually comprised of two elements: A perceived mismatch of demands and resources and the perception that the mismatch is too much to handle with calm and balanced pacing. Depending on how we respond, these dilemmas can set the stage for chronic stress. "What's really important is how you're reacting to [a stressor]. Something's a stressor if you perceive it as a stressor," says neuroscientist Jane Lubischer, Ph.D., of North Carolina State University. "What's stressful to one may not be to another."

In order to achieve a different response to one's dilemma, we must first understand it. Let's take a look at how these speedstress-inducing dilemmas unfold in real life.

Dilemma #1: Too much to do in too little time

After George W. Bush's top domestic policy advisor was arrested for stealing, the *New York Times* reported that the president commented "something went wrong in Claude Allen's life, and that is really sad." The "something" was this first demand-resource dilemma. As court records revealed, Mr. Allen had been putting in 14-hour workdays while being a parent to four young children. As if that were not enough, he had repeatedly moved households, and rarely got adequate sleep. Mr. Allen had become speedstressed. He had, he told the court, "lost perspective."

In this primary dilemma, using haste – and/or its variant, pushing through tasks without adequate breaks - seems to promise a reward: the closing of the gap between demands and resources. Certainly, that seemed logical to Rebecca* after the birth of her twins. "My memory of that period is just kind of 'go go go' and trying to have everything perfectly organized and set up. There was no downtime, or allowing myself any."

Rebecca's quest to have "everything perfectly organized" constituted her dilemma's demand, which existed in the context

of time's seeming lack as a resource. Rebecca has since identified that she held unrealistic expectations of herself during
that postnatal period. At the time, however, she acted as many
speedstressed people do: She treated time like a balloon, as if
the more to-dos she forced into an allotted period, the more it
would expand. (For those of you who, unlike Rebecca, truly can't
shrink the demand side of your dilemma, take heart: It is always
possible, as you'll see, to enhance your external and internal
resources. Rushing often makes us blind to this fact.)

The fear of falling behind if one doesn't move at a fast pace is
nearly universal among the speedstressed, especially among those
in this first dilemma who are still working. Stelle Shumann*, a
public relations manager, long believed in speedstress' necessity
in the workplace. "If you're not busy enough, is your job really
necessary? I wanted to be seen as very busy. I didn't want to lose
my job," recalls Stelle. "What can happen for some of us is that
we speed up in order to look busy."

This thinking seems reasonable on its face. Scratch beneath
the surface, however, and speed's protection morphs into flimsy
illusion. While it's true that being a dawdler on the job is never
advisable, it's undeniable that hard work didn't protect many of
the millions of people laid off in the recent past. No amount of
hurry will surmount the trickle-down of macroeconomic forces
into the workforce. (Nor, as we'll see, is it true that there are no
reasonable ways to slow down in the workplace.)

On the individual level, moving at near constant haste tires
us, leads to errors and accidents and, consequently, poorer work
performance. It also induces tension, irritation, and over-activation in mind and body, with our relationships and good judgment paying the price. These effects, as Mr. Allen discovered, are
more likely to harm one's job security than taking brief, discrete
breaks and doing one's best to log reasonable hours.

Attempting to rush the primary dilemma away is to succumb to speedstressed "logic" – often in the form of black and white thinking - that takes little to no account of the complexity and vulnerability of our human nature. Like it or not, when we are fatigued and over-activated we are, much like a balloon, liable to "pop" from the pressure.

In the second and third dilemmas, people aim to generate somewhat different rewards, but they end up living in a way that feels too fast or busy – for them. In the second dilemma, what working folks might consider a wonderful resource – an abundance of time – flips to a demand: Fill me!

Dilemma #2: Too much time with too little to do

Carol Shaw was laid off at a time in her pharmaceuticals career when she could easily have retired. Even so, she had a very hard time letting herself do less. Like many newly free of work, she was still accustomed to the speedstressed rhythms of her old job and the role they played in her identity. "I went through two years of totally feeling I didn't know which end was up," she recalls. "…I felt like I was floundering. I was all over the board. I was frantic, anxious." As a result, Carol took on an over-abundance of commitments, describing herself when we met as "in a frenetic place." Her "road" out of the second dilemma had, indeed, landed her in the first!

The second dilemma can arise for retirees and job-seekers alike as they experience distress at the loss of old roles. After his layoff as a chemist in a major corporation, says Daniel Scheck, "I would spend a lot time just wondering what I was going to do with myself for the day." The unfamiliar expanse of free time in each day can seem to echo with unsettling messages about one's productivity or identity.

The transition into retirement can also raise difficult questions about values and self-worth. Guilt may arise about not staying busy, or about having the financial wherewithal to survive without a job while others struggle. The simple, slower pleasures dreamed of while still employed – reading in the middle of the day, for example – can feel self-indulgent when put into practice.

For people in this second dilemma, the realization that lack of work is not, in its early stages, free of internal stress can be unsettling. Becoming overly busy, while not necessarily one's intention, is sometimes the immediate reaction to one's lack of ease with free time.

Dilemma #3: Too much expense for too little income

As I listened to a recent college graduate speak on the radio, I was filled with sadness. The woman was so young to be, as she put it, "addicted to working." Her student loans demanded a high monthly payment, and the market for well-paying positions was less than promising. As a result, she felt she had to hold down three jobs.

Due to our national financial meltdown, increasing numbers of people find themselves grappling with this third dilemma. The need to take on extra work can cause one to feel helpless to do anything but rush. You may well know retirees who hadn't expected to work in retirement but now schedule their leisure pursuits around part-time jobs. Driven by anxiety about their shrunken retirement funds, some retirees can find it harder to settle into their "golden years."

The unemployed, shorn of adequate income, have additional incentives to rush. Believing that job-searching "24-7," as one person put it, will more quickly yield employment, the laid-off may not take adequate breaks, arriving at interviews stressed, tired, or unprepared. Even job-seekers who do slow down may find it difficult to do so regularly if family members, beset by their own anxieties, question their leisure time. "He will kind of say, 'Well, what have you been doing all day?' You know, that kind of thing," recounts one interviewee of her husband. "…I've got to find something soon cause my husband's just going to go off the deep end."

All Roads Lead to One

As has likely become clear, the second and third dilemmas result in anxiety or financial needs that make one highly vulnerable to generating the primary dilemma, "too much to do in too little time."

No matter your reasons for living in haste, you can learn to relate anew to them, and to yourself. Doing so, you will discover that lessening the gap between your "too much" and "too little" can be achieved by many means other than rushing.

But, we move too quickly here, for speedstress, rather than its solution, is still in need of examination.

What's my slowlution?

⮞ Identify what speedstress-inducing dilemma(s) you are, or have been, in. What "too much" and "too little" have caused you to hurry?

⮞ Begin saying (or thinking) the phrase *"What's my slowlution?"* until it takes on a natural rhythm.

Chapter 2

Hurried and Harried:
The Speedstressed
Story of Life

*"One factor which may have contributed significantly
[to the fatal decision to launch space shuttle Challenger] ...
is the effect on managers of several days
of irregular working hours and insufficient sleep."*

~ Rogers Commission Report,
Appendix G, "Human Factor Analysis"

One afternoon, Christine O'Kelly received her company's highest award in recognition of her long hours and hard work. As Christine accepted the award, she had little idea that her "I felt like I could never stop" lifestyle was about to receive a jolt, but it was. When she picked up the phone to tell her husband about being honored, he, tired out by his own hasty pace, was asleep at home. They realized with horror that he had slept through the closing time at their children's day care.

After safely retrieving their children, Christine and her husband did not rush on from that impactful event. Rather, they attended to its meaning and effects. For Christine, that meant intentionally acknowledging the price her children were paying for their parents' harried pace. What mattered most, she realized, was raising her children well. "My kids are so important to me but they were taking a backseat to this job. It was not what I wanted. I've always wanted to be a great mom." Why, Christine wondered, was she working so "very, very hard to move up the ladder quick?"

Our culture has a great deal to do with the answer to that question. A 2012 American Psychological Association (APA) survey designated money, work, and the economy as our predominant stressors. Our virtual in-boxes are, quite literally, bottomless; demands, queries, and information manifest by the minute. A Gallup daily tracking poll conducted over 18 months found that 20 percent of non-working adults, 28 percent of workers, and 32 percent of working women reported not having enough time on the previous day to "get done what you needed to do." Lack of time was correlated to a near doubling in the frequency of experiencing "a lot of stress," as well as to a dip in personal satisfaction.

Academic competition also serves to fuel both students' and parents' pace. (Many a parent knows well the time-consuming nature of shuttling teens to extracurricular activities.) The notion that identity derives in large part from one's work or wealth can cause us to over-commit to the former. Our culture's exaltation of speed can't be overlooked, either, trumpeted as it is in the "race for" this or that, and in news about ever-faster communication. Negative judgments about slowness also inflate speed's seeming desirability. As Sarah** writes, "For most of my life, I've been encouraged to think that slowing down meant I was lazy and a less-than-contributing person. This, I feel, is counter-productive, but very powerful when learned at an early age."

** "Sarah" and "Sean" are names I designated for, respectively, the anonymous female and male respondents to a pace-of-life survey I conducted in 2006 via mail (to random addresses across the country) and email. These names are distinct from those of interviewees, so they always indicate an anonymous survey respondent as the source for the associated quote.

Speedstress' entwinement throughout our contemporary society makes itself known from every corner. It is honked from car horns, acted out in the pace of passing pedestrians, and broadcast in the tension of overworked colleagues. You can encounter speedstress in the person who searches for work late into the night, in physicians' hasty interruptions of patients, and in the body language of someone who says "I'm listening," but radiates an eagerness to move on.

Institutionally, we see haste woven into policies and policy-making: from Medicare legislation in the 1990's that had to be corrected because it was enacted hurriedly to banks that no longer check your addition when you make a deposit because, in the words of a teller I queried, "it takes too much time."

It was, in part, inevitable that we'd come to this. Our human mind would create its own extra-capable extension, computing technologies that have driven, or influenced, many of our cultural triggers for speedstress. In the last thirty-five years, computing speed has advanced while its hardware has downsized, with the result that these technologies have disseminated their rapid pace throughout our lives.

The enormity of this technological advance easily distracts from taking full measure of just how short its time span has been. Three and a half decades is but a micro-sliver of a micro-sliver (and on and on) of human evolutionary time. No part of us – whether physical, intellectual or spiritual – has had the chance to evolve to anywhere near the point where trying to keep up with technology's pace doesn't cost us dearly.

"Typically, there's an increase in negative mood when people have a stressor," says Shevaun D. Neupert, Ph.D., who, as an associate professor of Psychology, researches the impact of demand stressors such as *too much to do in too little time*. "[People] also tend to experience more physical health problems … Daily stressors are also not so great for memory performance."

Typical effects of speedstress, such as overcrowded schedules, deficient sleep, missed meals, and anxiety, while stress-inducing in their own ways, also affect the brain's neurotransmitter functioning. As a result, we become more vulnerable to developing and practicing habitual behaviors. Staying in an anxious hurry can soon become a vicious cycle.

Short of death, the deepest price that we pay for living on the run is living with little to no awareness of our personal reality. "I feel like I lost who I was because I became so busy with what I was doing," recalls Christine O'Kelly.

Why does this happen?

As any driver knows, when you push harder on the accelerator, the need to attend to the road intensifies. Speed demands management so, by extension, it demands our attention. Fast-paced daily activities require a narrow focus if we are not to make errors, miss important information, or misspeak (if we multitask, our focus widens, often to the point of ineffectiveness). Either way, intently focused on the speedy completion of what's "out there" – an attitude I call *Next!* – we forget to check in with the "in here" of our emotions, stress level, and physical needs – in short, with our personal reality. This unbalanced external focus not only compromises how we take care of ourselves but also how we experience others and the world around us.

As a result, the speedstressed regularly miss what's here and now or, at times, even dismiss it. "Sometimes I'd come home [to family] and I had a list and I'd continue in this driven mode to do the things on my list," Shelley Beason recalls with an edgy laugh as she looks back on her days working in healthcare.

Shelley's attitude would signal to family: "Don't tell me about anything that's not on the list!".

Many of life's powerful offerings – from subtle messages in loved ones' remarks to scenic vistas - are regularly lost to us when we live with our attention beamed on *Next!* Our creativity and insights, our dreams and yearnings, fall into darkness. Hurry prevents us recognizing both external resources for dealing with our dilemma and the full range of our mental, emotional, and creative capabilities. This restricted awareness easily reinforces the belief that our primary resource for dealing with the demand-side of our dilemma lies in the pace we keep. Yet, in our modern age, haste tires us out and the tasks keep coming, so the gap between *too much* and *too little* remains.

Happily, accepting this reality will direct you in exactly the direction you need to go: inside, to begin making new choices. As we'll explore, slowing down allows you to recognize a wider range of internal and external resources with which to address your demands in a more balanced, creative, and effective manner. While your daily inflow of tasks will likely never be fully under your control, the choice to look to yourself for more sustainable solutions and approaches always is. No to-do list or boss can strip that ability away from you.

After their period of reflection, Christine O'Kelly and her husband decided to move away from their city home in order to provide a different life for themselves and their children. Yet, even after settling in a small town many miles to the east, Christine still had to make careful internal choices in order to slow down. "I knew I was going to go through some kind of withdrawal process. I first had to stop believing that somebody else was in control of my life, like an employer," says Christine.

Control, as it turns out, has a great deal to do with both speedstress and slowing down.

What's my slowlution?

﹩ How would you describe your experience of speedstress? Think about its physical, emotional and spiritual effects on you. How has it affected your plans, relationships, home- and work-life? (If judgment arises, call on kindness: Our culture makes tension and haste seem normal.) Begin to reframe any costs you notice into motivations for change. Write those motivations down.

﹩ Become alert to how you, and others, talk about stressors and pace-of-life. For instance, notice your and others' body language and vocabulary during such discussions. Do these communications engender positive feelings, or negative ones? A sense of personal control, or not? Again, just notice, without judgment.

Chapter 3

The Illogical "Logic" of Speedstress

"You get the anxiety because you are speeding up so much …
you feel like you're in a circle and there's no getting off …
VOOM! VOOM! VOOM!"

~ Stelle Shumann

Mariah Darlington remembers the ringing of a long-ago bell. Now, the sound reaches back across 70 years, but, back then, it called out across meadows, reaching a wet and happy Mariah as she dammed the creek on her childhood farm. Making a big pool was "the beginning and the end of life. It was just wonderful," recalls Mariah. "I'd hear the bell ringing for lunch and I'd say, 'When I grow up, I'm going to be able to just stay down here as long as I want and nobody's going to call me.'"

Nobody's going to call me… Don't we all long for that, even now?

In a speedstressed society, we get caught in a bind as we mature. We become capable and, therefore, responsible; others expect, and often deserve, our attention and follow-through. All this is well and good – until we fall prey to the illogic and denial of cultural messages that tell us we can – and must - stay on the go to an extreme extent. You know these messages: Marketing that touts sugar- and caffeine-laden energy drinks as the answer for depleted energy; the boss whose assignments pile up into an unspoken demand that you work late or skip lunch; the radio DJ who defines having a few moments to "sit around" as a "waste," as I heard one day.

Such messages tell us that Mariah's early needs and longings – and yours – fell away with childhood; that our desires for play, creativity and connection, for rest and quiet-time, are just that: desires, rather than needs. As such, they easily seem expendable in the face of productivity's demands. Those longings, though, remind us that slow times helped us feel fully in, or present to, our life. As adults, such experiences are still essential to both nurturing and expressing our humanness.

There's nothing wrong with either our obligations or our human wants and needs, of course. Problems arise only when the balance between the two is not right for us. Speedstress' unspoken illogical "logic", which equates rushing through tasks with solving our anxiety about those tasks, pushes us toward such an imbalance. This "solve the dilemma ⟶ solve the anxiety" thinking might not pose a problem – if a dilemma arose only occasionally. However, let's see how this "logic" plays out when demands don't cease, as in Dave Banner's life.

Speedstressed "Logic"

Too much to do in too little time ⟶ anxiety ⟶

Pick up your pace ⟶ get more done ⟶ dilemma is resolved ⟶

Anxiety lessens or disappears.

As the executive's previous description of his day made clear, he regularly lives with "too much to do in too little time." So, he rushes, feeling like he has no choice but to do so. You may have noticed Dave's plaintive queries at the start of Chapter 1: "When is there time … When do you relax … When are you allowed?" As Dave's haste has become habitual, he's lost a sense of control over his life. He is far from alone. Speedstressed living is often experienced as a circling wheel from which there is no apparent exit. (Mariah's reference to a "treadmill" is similar to the terms "vicious cycle" and "hamster wheel," which other interviewees used.) Feeling out of control of both one's demands and one's pace of life is central to the experience of being speedstressed.

Here we find the first illogic of speedstress, for research has long told us that a perceived lack of control causes stress, which we most frequently experience as anxiety. And yet, that is the very emotion we hope – whether consciously or unconsciously - to lessen by rushing through our obligations!

Looking at speed of movement in its most literal sense brings us around to lack of control yet again. As our pace quickens, we are more likely to trip and fall, lose things, or have an accident - unless we remain vigilant throughout, a difficult achievement in our distracting modern era. Our haste and task-focus also prevent a thoughtful consideration of alternate solutions to our dilemmas. Without such options in mind, it's all too easy to lapse into a sense of helplessness about doing anything other than staying on the run.

If our dilemmas were finite, we would likely avoid feeling so out of control. We would live more in accordance with our natural rhythms, expending bursts of energy and then slowing down again, achieving a state of dynamic balance. But our modern age changes the game, ensuring that demands tug constantly at many of us. Tasks keep piling in, despite our resort to a hasty pace. And, of course, when one's *too much-too little dilemma* is driven by psychological factors such as a perceived need to outpace others, or a fear of one's emotions, the habit of overfilling one's life receives a constant recharge.

Speedstressed, we expend our energy, and our anxious pace cuts us off from our calmer center, diminishing access to our gifts and abilities. In rushing, we rush by ourselves. Consequently, we experience ourselves as less of a resource in relation to our demands, thus making the gap between our *too much* and *too little* feel that much larger.

Until we begin to address the only aspect of our demand-resource dilemma that we can control – ourselves as resource - the denial of our need for balance will continue to exact a toll. As it is, we often normalize these costs; after all, we witness them occurring in others' lives. "People minimize the impact of sleep deprivation, skipping meals, social isolation, or different stressors, too, like family stress, work stress," notes psychiatrist Catherine Soriano.

To counter that minimization, let's dive straight into the middle of Stelle Shumann's experience of speedstress. For Stelle, fulfilling the demands of Fortune 500 companies meant that: "You speed up and you're rushing around and you're thinking about all these things so your heart rate goes faster, you might breathe more shallow and you're moving faster, and that sends a signal to your brain, 'Uh oh, something's going wrong here,'" says Stelle.

The Illogic of Speedstress

Anxious hurry

- heightens tense activation

- decreases sense of control

- diminishes awareness of the present moment

- encourages time-consuming errors and missteps

- denies the reality that new tasks will arrive

- depletes inner resources – energy, calm thinking, and recognition of new coping methods

...resulting in more stressors, anxiety, and tension.

Something's going wrong here.

Stelle's phrasing clearly conveys her anxiety. But what exactly serves as the catalyst that converts haste to anxiety?

The answer, in a word, is this: activation.

The speedier our motions, whether keeping pace with technology or moving our bodies through space, the more activated our "biopsychological" system becomes, as psychologist and researcher Robert Thayer, Ph.D., describes it. For example, think about two people passing each other in a hallway: one walks leisurely, while the other's pace seems to signal, "I'm late to an important meeting." Both people would experience activation, but the rushed individual, notes Thayer, "would be expending more energy at a rapid pace and be more activated under those circumstances."

Dr. Thayer's research has led him to conclude that two interacting dimensions of arousal, or activation, influence moods. "Energetic" activation refers to one's level of energy, in all its gradations down to tiredness. "Tense" activation encompasses physical and emotional tension, ranging from calmness to tension. These dimensions are reflected in both physiological changes (hence, *bio*) and in our personal experiencing (*psychological*). In Thayer's book *Calm Energy*, he diagrams these two dimensions of activation ("calmness-tension" and "energy-tiredness") as lines that intersect, resulting in four differing quadrants of activation.

CALM ENERGY	TENSE ENERGY
CALM TIREDNESS	TENSE TIREDNESS

Based on graph in Thayer, Robert E. *Calm Energy: how people regulate mood with food and exercise.* New York: Oxford University Press, 2001., p.91

It will likely come as little surprise that "tense energy" and "tense tiredness" are the types of biopsychological activation we experience when we are too much on the run. But how does tense activation nudge haste into anxiety?

Research shows that our physical experience, which includes our pace, can influence our mental or emotional state - for better or worse. For instance, half-smiling can brighten one's mood. Striking a pose that conveys power for two minutes can cause an internal experience of empowerment, as well as an increase in the release of testosterone. This interconnectedness of mind and body is aptly reflected in some of the descriptors Dr. Thayer uses on his "Activation-Deactivation Adjective Check List." For example, "jittery … clutched-up … stirred-up … sluggish" can each refer to bodily or mental/emotional states.

Speedstress' illogic, its tendency to work against its supposed reward, arises in part from the increased muscle tension, accelerated heartbeat, or quicker breathing that can come into play when we move quickly. While such physical changes can certainly occur under positive circumstances – while exercising, for example - they are also associated in our brain with anxiety. Therefore, the margin between moving at a hasty pace in order to lessen one's anxiety, and potentially increasing it, is a very narrow one.

We may initially respond to our dilemma with an energized fast pace and a low degree of tension (*low* tension can actually increase our energy and focus). However, if, over time, our tension climbs, or our pace is inadequately balanced by rest or relaxation, we will become tired. And that has consequences. "When energy decreases, when resources decrease, and more is demanded of you, it's a source of anxiety," says Dr. Thayer.

It's easy to see how speedstress, the antidote for anxiety, only creates more. Sadly, as you probably know all too well, the consequences of keeping up a tense and hasty pace don't stop there. The quote opening this chapter alludes to the ultimate price astronauts paid after the decision to launch the space shuttle Challenger was made by NASA's tense, over-tired managers and contractors. As fallible human beings, we often don't attend, drive, act, or think well when we're tired, anxious, or moving too fast.

Accuracy certainly suffers when we stay at speed. Researchers have long studied what they call the "speed-accuracy trade-off" in which our accuracy of movement declines the faster we do it. As if that weren't enough, tense activation and speed can spin off a wide range of unexpected consequences, as Zelda Lockhart experienced several years back.

Zelda, then a working single mother who was also taking college courses, placed her son in his car-seat one late afternoon. "I was rushing," says Zelda. "I was like 'I've got to get home, got to make dinner, and put him to bed, got to study' … I was thinking way ahead." Zelda placed her son in his seat and, then, inadvertently locked the car - with her keys inside.

When we are focused on *Next!* our mind races ahead and we lose awareness of our physical experience in the present, the body's sole time zone. As a result, we make mistakes, misplace things, take in directions and assignments incompletely, or blurt out what's on the tip of our tongues. In the end, haste and tense activation only boost our anxiety and cost us time.

As is probably clear by now, the "stress" in "speedstress'" refers as much to the problems that result from staying too much on the run as it does to the anxiety generated by a *too much-too little dilemma*. So: Why do we keep up such a problematic pace? As we'll explore next, haste can become habitual, meaning that slowing down, for all its appeal, can be challenging to achieve.

What's my slowlution?

➰ Recall incidents in which trying to save time has actually cost you (for example, being stopped for speeding, taking a tumble, etc.).

➰ Moving too fast for too long makes us vulnerable to heightened stress and decreased energy. How has this manifested in your life?

Chapter 4

Dug In: Speedstress as Habit

"I have been able to break some other bad habits in the past,
and so I think if someone would have said [a rushed pace]
was a habit, maybe that would have helped."

~ Shelley Beason

Feeling too tense and over-activated to head home after a day at work with top executives, Stelle Shumann would unwind at the mall. "I found I couldn't just come off from rushing around into calming down. I didn't have the tools for it," she recalls. Soon, no part of Stelle's week afforded respite. "On your weekends you're running around and everything's rush, rush, rush, rush, rush, rush. You're so hooked into it," she says.

A fast pace, kept up, soon keeps us.

Stelle's use of the word "hooked" is telling: Speedstress can become habitual; it certainly had for Stelle. You'll recall that her original trigger for rushing was her anxiety about being fired if she was viewed as not busy enough. Yet, here she describes hurrying through her weekends, when her boss wasn't present and work wasn't expected of her. Stelle rushed because it had become her default behavior, or habit. If you've tried to slow down and experienced anxiety that prevented change, or if you've suddenly found yourself right back in your tasks again, speedstress may well have become a habit for you.

Once a habit is established, its automatic nature often shuts down our awareness of it. We don't think about our behavior or the beliefs driving it, we simply do it. Like dry, hard-packed soil that resists a shovel's attempt to turn it, habits require the "rain" of our attention on them before change can occur. Often, the costs that result from turning to one-note behavioral responses in a dynamic world (including our own biopsychological universe) are what first prompt us to offer such awareness.

In this chapter, we'll explore five elements as lenses through which you can explore speedstress' habitual nature: triggers, the recurring behavior, reward(s), craving, and belief(s).

Of course, no one likes to think of her- or himself as having unhelpful behaviors, much less habitual ones; yet, we all succumb at one point or another. So, treat yourself with kindness as you read on. You might also want to foster change by considering how each element might serve as a doorway into reshaping your pace.

Triggers

What stimulates us to develop and practice a habitual behavior? In the case of speedstress, there are *three universal triggers*.

1. *The dilemma*

As we've discussed, a *too much–too little dilemma*, with its perceived or actual mismatch between demands and

Prelude to Change

Identify how the elements of habit apply to your pattern of staying on the run or over-booking:

- *Triggers* – what sets you on the run?

- Your speed-stressed *behaviors* in addition to your anxious hurry.

- The *rewards* you desire or "crave" (whether consciously or unconsciously) from speedstress.

- The *beliefs* driving your anxious pace.

33

resources, is the precipitating trigger. Haste seems the obvious solution.

2. *Anxiety*

Our perception of the dilemma is anxiety-producing. Anxiety, our felt experience of stress, can range in intensity from uncomfortable to highly distressing. Because anxiety makes us ill at ease, it serves its evolutionary purpose well, priming us to flee from threat. Unlike physical threats, however, our modern dilemma doesn't crash away into the underbrush; it's with us much of the time, setting the stage for ongoing anxiety that we try to quell by hurrying.

3. *Over-activation of body and mind*

This trigger comes into play after living at a fast pace has become an established pattern. It's common for someone who lives on the run to wake up with mind and body set to "Go!" mode, irrespective of his or her exhaustion. Says journalist Rhonda Miller, "I always slept well and I slept deeply, but I always felt like I was sleeping fast." Tension, or a feeling of being over-stimulated, becomes the norm and, as such, is often unnoticed as a trigger in its own right.

Your unique triggers

There are also triggers unique to your life that you have – consciously or unconsciously - come to associate with your dilemma; for example, a time of day, the weight of your briefcase, or the sight of your office door. For Eric Truran, a small-business owner, self-talk did the trick. His customary reaction to a mismatch between his task list and his time was "It's busy! Oh my god, I better get busy!" Unsurprisingly, that inner lingo sparked him right into action – without any thought about how to work more calmly and efficiently.

For those on the other end of the employment spectrum, circumstances such as an impending lunch date with a former co-worker might trigger you to fill your calendar so that you'll have things to report. As we saw earlier, Carol Shaw's anxiety after being separated from her job became a driver in causing her to over-commit, but a trigger unique to her personality propelled her, as well. Carol is, she tells me, a person more comfortable "doing, versus thinking."

Only you can define the unique triggers that join with your dilemma and anxiety to propel your pace during the course of any day. To identify them, become a gentle detective. Resolve to notice when you are hurrying (use notes to remind yourself to do so). As soon as you become aware of your pace, see if you can identify what triggered it. Ask yourself: *What was I doing? Where was I? What thoughts or feelings was I having? What sounds or sights did I notice? Who was present?*

Because your hasty pace is established, your unique triggers may not be immediately evident. Be patient and persistent, and be sure to celebrate even the slightest of clues. Identifying your triggers will allow you to recognize them more quickly, providing you the choice to respond differently.

The habitual behavior

This element of habit is its actual practice, whether as a behavior, a thought pattern, or a regular routine. In the case of speedstress, moving anxiously at haste through tasks constitutes the central habitual behavior. Yet, there are likely many other ways you put speedstress into action.

Enter once again the gentle detective. Notice, for instance, how quickly you talk when you're hurrying. How well do you listen? Do you tell others to hurry? Do you stop to think when someone asks something of you, or do you automatically say "Yes?" When someone keeps you longer than you want, do you frequently feel impatient? How does your body signal your tension: For example, do you bob your knees up and down or thrum your fingers?

Become aware, as well, of routine behaviors that express, or support, your haste or intent focus on tasks. Speedstressed classics include multi-tasking, regularly skipping meals or eating quickly; going to bed late and, of course, working late. Perhaps you find yourself repeatedly putting off get-togethers with friends, or telling yourself that you'll let yourself rest after getting "one more thing done."

The repetition of any behavior weaves a reinforcing message through our psyches. In the case of speedstress, that message is shot through with circular reasoning: *If I'm hurrying so much, hurrying must be essential.* The familiarity of habit, in other words, breeds not contempt, but a belief in its necessity. As a result, it becomes difficult to identify, or even consider, new responses to "too much to do in too little time."

Once you do begin to alter your pace, your speedstressed patterns of behavior will try to reassert themselves. You might think of anxiety as the psyche's first salvo in this power struggle. The brain reads the familiar as safe, and reacts with anxiety to change or novelty, which it sees as problematic – even if it's good for us. In the case of speedstress, anxiety poses a double challenge because it served as a trigger in its own right for the behavior we want to lessen.

Eric Truran observed habit's tenacity after he moved from Cambridge to the hills of Vermont. Friends from the city came to visit him and his wife Diana Salyer. After several months of consciously slowing down, Eric recognized how "wound up" his visitors were. And Diana noticed that, even though their friends were miles removed from any external triggers, their habit of staying busy kept asserting itself. She recalls her visitors' typical morning greeting, "'So, what's the plan?' … They didn't want to sit around and relax."

Had Diana asked her friends why a plan was necessary, I'd bet they wouldn't have had a reason to offer that was relevant to the here-and-now of their visit to Vermont. In fact, when asked to explain habitual routines, many of us resort to responses along the lines of, "I do it because … well, it's just what I do."

Reward(s)

Rewards are crucial to the development of habits: Without perceiving at least one benefit or reward from a behavior, we won't practice it enough to make it habitual. Rewards are either positive in nature - what our hasty pace seems to carry us toward ("personal and professional approval," as one interviewee told me) – or they offer an avoidance of a real or imagined negative outcome ("falling behind" is commonly cited in relation to speedstress).

Most speedstressed people hope to receive two rewards from hurrying through the day:

1. *A lessening of one's dilemma*

2. *A reduction in anxiety about the dilemma*

Yet, the potency of these goodies – which can be real or, merely, perceived – fades due to today's ongoing influx of to-dos. As Stelle Shumann puts it, "No matter how fast you work and no matter how much you do, it's never enough and it's not good enough."

Your unique rewards

Like triggers, rewards can be highly individual. "Wow, I had a really good day!" Rhonda Miller used to say to herself after checking off a number of to-dos. A sense of high productivity can become reinforcing in and of itself. Rewards can also accrue as hopes and beliefs. For instance, a relentless push to find work may foster the belief that new employment is imminent. These rewards aren't bad in and of themselves; they become problematic only when they are unrealistic, or reinforcing of unhelpful behaviors.

What unique rewards do you cull from living at haste? Perhaps you have a boss who praises you every time you work late, or you treat yourself by purchasing a box of candies. Take careful note, and inquire. Are the benefits you're running towards really present? If they are, are they truly helpful to you? Often, habit carries us unknowingly past the "end-dates" of rewards. If you stay at haste, will you have the energy to enjoy any benefits that do result? Examine whether you assume the future with unrealistic certainty.

And, be sure to take an inventory of all the costs you may be suffering due to a hasty over-focus on tasks. Habits, by their nature, aren't flexible or adaptive to the ever-changing circumstances of life. Consequently, they usually begin to exact a price.

Rhonda's slowing down process has gone on long enough that she can recognize the costs hurry incurs. "At the same time you're rushing, you're really not getting all the richness of every moment, which is really life," she says.

Now, Rhonda recognizes that, while hurry is sometimes necessary, slowing down is often possible. She makes a point of noticing its rewards, from the delight of walking her dog with awareness to an appreciation of nature's beauty.

Craving

As we gain some rewards from a habitual behavior, we begin wanting, whether consciously or not, to re-experience them. You've probably noticed a craving when you've denied yourself, or missed out on, an enjoyable and customary behavior – say, eating the usual doughnut with your morning coffee.

Craving provides the *oomph* that keeps one riding speed-stress' seemingly unceasing wheel. It is the activated, but often imperceptible, desire to resolve our dilemma, avoid the imagined consequences of not doing so, and/or lessen our anxiety. Without such a desire, we probably wouldn't keep up a taxing pace.

Once it's developed initially, craving is re-activated as soon as a trigger for our habitual behavior arises. Cravings can continue to drive a habit long after its rewards have ceased and its costs have mounted. This is because habit's fifth element, beliefs, can substitute for actual rewards.

Beliefs

We can think of beliefs as the "stories" we make up to explain the world around us, and our place in it. Habitual behaviors are by definition inflexible, so we can assume that the beliefs underlying them are as well. Rhonda offers an example of how a rigid belief can affect our pace of life. "Nobody ever thinks they have money to slow down. Everybody thinks that it's all about money." Often black and white in nature (notice Rhonda's "all about"), these perceptions and beliefs become rigid once we become too caught up in habit to question their validity.

Unsurprisingly, the application of inflexible beliefs to life's ever-shifting realities often doesn't result in effective or positive outcomes. It can take a while to notice this, however, when we're on autopilot. Consequently, we can end up running *from* our dilemma or *to* our reward based on what we *believe* to be true about one or the other.

As we'll discuss in later chapters, slowing down will require the revision of any beliefs you hold about haste's unquestionable necessity. Rhonda set about slowing down only after she came to believe that she couldn't do otherwise. "If it's something you have to do, you just have to figure out some other way," she says. "Even though all the signs and all the reasonable people and all the money and all the budgets point to that fact that you're not going to be able to do it, if you want to do it, you'll figure it out."

You will, indeed.

What's my slowlution?

⮑ Think about the five elements as doorways into slowing down. Which door feels most open to you? How would you like to take a first step through it? (Ex: Reworking a triggering belief, or gradually removing an unhealthy reward.)

⮑ If you feel anxious haste has become a habit, draw out your habit loop and post it nearby: dilemma ⟶ anxiety (+ any other triggers) ⟶ *hasty pace* (+ any other habitual behaviors) ⟶ actual/believed diminishment of dilemma/anxiety (+ any other rewards) ⟶ craving (for more rewards) ⟶ *hasty pace* ⟶ ...

At Garden's Edge

Revaluing Slowness

Chapter 5

The Power of Pacing

"Everything touches everything."

~ Jolene Robinson, R.N.,
on our biochemistry

We begin with an act of thievery.

I committed the act while giving a talk on slowing down, and I did it without straying an inch from my appointed place at a bookstore's lectern. I simply introduced myself and, without hesitation or explanation, began rapidly reading Mary Oliver's poem "When I Am Among the Trees." The poem, as some of you may know, illuminates the gift of living slowly and with awareness, yet I read it as fast as I could without skipping any words. When I finished, I re-read the verses at a normal cadence and, so, with the appropriate intonations.

Afterwards, I asked for feedback about the rushed first reading. One attendee's comment was typical, "It was hard to follow what you were saying. I kind of followed it, but I couldn't really enjoy the poem and it took away from my understanding of it."

Took away. The pace at which I spoke had robbed those listening to me. As I rattled through Oliver's verses, the audience members' intent efforts to make out individual words prevented them from enjoying the poem's lyricism. Nor were they able to translate Oliver's references to trees into their own desires and experiences.

Our own pacing and that all around us shapes our experience, perceptibly or imperceptibly, entering us through the portals of hearing, sight, touch, and sensation. Near-constant contractions exhaust a laboring woman, even as they signal the need for heightened vigilance by her birth team. Police cars streaking down the street cause us to turn and wonder, while a bedmate's slower, softer utterances let us know that he or she is edging into sleep. Indeed, different tempos – for instance, the long-gone newsboy's call, a stretching "read" just before the patter of "all about it" - become nothing less than cultural signatures.

It is no more possible to remove pacing from our experience of life than it is to remove tides from the ocean or stop-and-go rhythms from rush hour traffic. Yet, here we come to a paradox: Exactly because pacing is to be found everywhere, we often accord it the attention we give air, which is to say, next to none. So, let us pause to offer it the examination it deserves, beginning in the animal kingdom, where many of us are more apt to recognize the interdependent relationship of pacing, balance, and sustainability.

The power of a paced cycling between slowness and action is highlighted by a bear's active foraging for food during summer and fall, followed by his reduced energy expenditure as he hibernates through the winter. We see this necessary cycling, too, in the descent of birds into marshlands for rest as they journey between seasons and latitudes.

As always, sustainability depends on balance. No one knows this better than a jockey. Any jockey worth his salt shapes his progress down a track in this dynamic fashion, at times urging the horse on, or holding it back. As they proceed, jockeys attend closely to their horses' cues and energy, as well as to their position among the other horses, and the track's distance and condition. Winning is about far more than running full speed for the length of the track. It is a dynamic balancing act of pace and energy, pace and position.

Much the same can be said for us.

Moving forward effectively and sustainably through life requires regularly moderating our pace according to both external circumstances *and* personal experience. Our biopsychological need for balance asks us to match the pursuit of a deadline with some rest and quiet, to replenish our energy by taking in food. When we regularly over-focus on doing, we lose touch with our need for this dynamic back and forth. Our body's cycles and rhythms whir on, but at a cost, for to live unbalanced is to go against our very design.

Second by second, round the clock, our exquisitely intercon-nected biochemistry, paced largely to the unceasing rise and fall of light, is at work throughout our delicate tissues and organs. *Delicate.* It's important not to rush by this word, this truth about us. Speedstressed pacing conspires with our cloaking skin to ob-scure our inner vulnerability. We easily forget that poor nutrition, tension, or lack of sleep affect our finely balanced biochemistry and the "ground" in which it works, our spongy, fragile tissues.

Consider the vital cycling of blood gases taking place inside you right now. The exchange of oxygen and carbon dioxide is occurring in capillaries so narrow that red blood cells must pass through in single file, their walls a mere cell's width in thickness. Consider this, too: Your processing of these words relies on nerve signals that traverse networks far more delicate than the finest

lace. On these, and many other slender threads, our biopsychological balance rises and falls.

Woven of cycles and feedback loops, our biochemical system
invites resilience. Yet its delicacy and interconnection also invites
danger, for one imbalance can cascade into another. Our stress
cycle offers a vital example of this.

As we've seen, the stress process begins in our mind, as we
weigh our resources against our demands, and find the former
lacking. As a result, we feel anxiety, even threat. Sensing this,
the brain's hypothalamus "telegraphs" the adrenals, glands
perched like caps atop the kidneys, and they respond by releas-
ing the stress hormone epinephrine. We are most concerned
with cortisol, however. It is excreted in the second round of the
body's response, when our stress doesn't quickly pass. Then, the
hypothalamus takes action for a second time, sending chemical
messengers, via the pituitary, down to the adrenals. They stimu-
late cortisol's release into the bloodstream, its pathway to the brain.

Our body's design would have us experience only brief
elevations of circulating stress hormones. Chronic stress, by
definition, upsets this pacing. If cortisol remains in the bloodstream too long it has toxic effects, leading to everything from
insulin resistance to high blood pressure to lowered immunity.
"If you have [cortisol] elevation and maintain it, instead of being
in surges…," says neuroscientist Jane Lubischer, "then you start
having deleterious effects, including loss of neurons in the brain."

Dr. Lubischer refers specifically to the loss of hippocampal
neurons. Unfortunately, these are the very brain cells that register
that the blood's cortisol level is adequate, triggering a reduction
in its release. With some of these cells harmed by cortisol, says
Dr. Lubischer, "What's happened to your negative feedback?
You've lost some of it. So now you've made things even worse,

because you don't have as strong a negative feedback in your system, so it's harder to bring those cortisol levels back down."

As a result, a chronic stress response can remain over-activated. Over time, exhaustion can mask our felt experience of this tense activation. Chronic stress' negative influence is often magnified by typical speedstressed behaviors, such as eating fast-food or forgoing exercise. The resulting biochemical effects cascade into seemingly unrelated processes. For example, when the sleep cycle is thrown off, functions as diverse as blood-sugar regulation, appetite regulation, and the production of glycogen to fuel the brain are impacted.

Your many inner workings may seem as dim and distant as the ocean floor, yet they are as real as the rise and fall of your chest. So, attend when your body speaks to you; it's no thief. The body's intention is to restore us to the balance and inner rhythms that support our well-being.

What's my slowlution?

⪦ Make your inner life real. If "Bodies - The Exhibit" comes to your town, go, or look at images on-line. Read up about your body's feedback loops.

⪦ Begin to notice all the ways that living systems rely on balance, on the recurrence of rhythms. For instance, both too much water, or too little, can cause plants to die. Or, take close note of how your body tugs at you for rest after a physically active day.

Chapter 6

The Necessity of Slowness

"Take rest; a field that has rested gives a bountiful crop."

~ Ovid

The breeze causes orange-gold leaves to rise and fall like small sighs that drift downward toward the pond behind my house. Ducks glide across the water, quacking as others appear, making a dark wedge in the blue sky. Enticed by the shining circle below, the birds begin gliding downwards. Yet, in their final moments of descent, they tilt slightly away from their watery haven, as if they are fighting their own decision to come to rest. I realize they are braking so as to glide safely onto the water, rather than suffer a hard landing

Slowing down is a necessity, a fact as true for us as for those ducks. A man we'll call Evan will help to highlight this important reality.

Evan owned and managed a business, so he found it very difficult to take vacations, says his leadership and career coach, Joan Roberts Eastman. In this, Evan was much like those ducks tilting away from that glistening pond; unlike them, however, he didn't intend to ease into rest. Over decades, Evan worked doggedly and with all good intention until, in middle age, he had a nervous breakdown so severe that he had to be hospitalized.

Evan had what, in vehicular terms, we would call an accident. Like many of us, he had a harder time accepting his own need to "brake" than he did that of the 3,000-pound mass of metal he called his car! Yet, the reality is this: If we are to rebalance away from tense and tired over-activation, we often have no choice but to, quite literally, slow our pace.

Why do I say this?

While speed tends to shift us toward tense activation, slowing down moves us toward calm. Any readers who are parents know this, for few children downshift from raucous play into sleep without an intervening period of calm – be it a warm bath or a softly-spoken story. Moreover, slow's soothing powers don't fade in adulthood; rather, they provide researched benefits.

What's my slowlution?

Slower

- Calm
- Soothe
- Distract from stressful dilemma
- Replenish energy

Faster

- Distract
- Promote enjoyment, connection
- Revitalize energy

... with the fullest focus possible

Patients who sit calmly for five minutes before their blood pressure is taken can decrease the systolic (upper number) pressure in their arteries by as much as 14 points. Meditation and slow, deep breathing can benefit our mood and immune system. Naps, those most luxurious of slowlutions, have a powerful effect in less than half an hour, boosting performance by as much as 34 percent. Wakeful breaks from lifting activities, if long enough, prove invaluable to replenishing muscles with oxygen and thus decreasing vulnerability to injury.

Yet, as anyone who's gone through a post-lunch slump in the workplace knows, "fast" slowlutions have their own merit as well. Here, the emphasis is on either revitalizing one's energy or slowing down *from* stressors, rather than literally. These types of slow-downs (as I'll refer to slowlutions from time to time) can also address speedstress' isolating over-focus on to-dos. Faster ways to slow down might include playing a game, calling a funny friend, or briskly moving one's body.

Whether fast or slow, taking breaks according to your present needs can shift you away from tension and tiredness toward the "calm energy" quadrant Dr. Thayer described. A sense of energized calm – or, simply, getting closer to it - allows us to focus better and to feel more absorbed in our experience in the moment, which is to say, in our life.

In part, this is because our psyches translate increased calm to mean a diminishment, or absence, of threat. On a conscious level, we feel more confident and are less likely to interpret circumstances as stressful. As our perception of stress declines over time, our biochemical stress response can as well, lessening cortisol's toxic effects.

Our biopsychological system, in short, exhales at a slower pace and our mood rises when we are more rested or energized. Emotional positivity, in turn, helps broaden our thinking, allowing us greater access to our creativity and problem-solving skills. Given this, it's not surprising that Dr. Thayer believes that "calm energy" allows us to produce our highest quality work.

A slower pace also provides us the ability to act deliberately and with forethought. Our legal system harnesses this capacity, tasking juries with carrying out an unhurried review of the evidence – deliberating, rather than rushing through. Even the action-packed arena of sport draws on slowness: Contested moves are reviewed not in fast-forward, but in slow motion. (Imagine the outcry from fans if they weren't!)

When Jane Lubischer first started to study tai chi, her instructor provided a vivid lesson in the care-full experiencing and close examination a slower pace affords. "My teacher had us start by saying 'make a fist'," recalls Jane, "and we all made a fist. He said, 'I challenge you. I don't think you know how to make a fist. You don't know what you just did.' He said, 'OK, now open your hand and make a fist as slowly as you possibly can and watch: Which finger moves first? Which one should go first, do they all go together? At what speed?'"

Jane's teacher was inviting his students to direct their attention to more than their fist-making. He wanted them to become fully aware by noting how they related to what was happening. While hurry often transits us like an elevated railway above both our inner life and external events, slowing down allows us to notice what's happening right here, right now.

Where our alert attention meets the present, a flash of insight or awareness often arises, expanding the moment beyond the commonplace, beyond the simple sum of *in here* and *out there*. Slow's greatest power rests in this alchemy; much like gold, it makes possible a heightened internal conductivity to wisdom and other riches.

When we apply this lens of heightened awareness to the common speedstressed sentiment, "Whatever I do, it's never enough," the implied reference to one's tasks or workload recedes, and a deeper meaning arises. The lament speaks to how much of ourselves we leave behind when we live too fast for our own comfort; how thin the fabric of our awareness becomes. Only when we slow down to invite awareness can we come to know our own values and attitudes, our bodily, emotional and spiritual callings. Only then can we make the intentional choices – large and small - that bring how we live more into alignment with *who* we are.

Had Joan's friend Evan earlier become aware of the importance of aligning his pace of life with the reality of his acute need for rest, he would, like the ducks on that autumn day, have avoided a hard landing. But he, like all of us, had to actively learn the lessons he needed.

Fortunately, Evan's enforced rest made slow's necessity obvious. "It's such an irony," Joan says, "that before the nervous breakdown he did not think he could run his business by slowing down. Now he realizes he can't run his business by *not* slowing down."

What's my slowlution?

≋ Enlist a friend: For one minute, walk together very quickly while one of you talks and the other listens. Switch roles and repeat. Slow down and talk about your hurried experiences as listener and talker. What's different at your slower pace?

≋ Think back to times when slowing down has proven powerful. Keep your eyes open for its benefit in the present.

Chapter 7

Self-ish versus Selfish:
Slow's Enriching Effect on Others

"If you don't take care of yourself, you cannot help anybody else."

~ Ian Florian

We've been focusing on slowing down in the context of individual needs and experiences. So, right about now, a niggling doubt may be surfacing in you: *Isn't this 'me-focus' a bit much?* Greet such doubt kindly, for its appearance is entirely understandable.

Our culture venerates speed, while self-care often demands slowing down. When we are pulled between these two competing influences, a list of unfinished to-dos can tip the balance toward staying busy. Valuing ourselves over tasks and, at times, over our children, can spark internal messages of selfishness (or, in the workplace, of disloyalty).

Yet, if we stop to count the costs that hurry and an ongoing focus on tasks impose on others, a far different conclusion emerges. "There's a certain vibe of expediency and urgency that lead to – they're trade-offs," says social activist Claudia Horwitz. "The faster people think they have to do things, the less conscious … we are of the fall-out. I think it manifests in a lot of ways … I think often it leads to carelessness, on many levels, including how we treat people."

Small moments of kindness and connection fall by the wayside when we are rushed and anxious. We listen less well, inadvertently inviting misunderstandings and resentments. Anniversaries, birthdays, and other special occasions are more easily overlooked. The loss of personal encounters, whether pillow talk or an expression of appreciation to a friend, whittles away at closeness over time.

When we do slow down to be with loved ones, our bodies may be fully present, but our minds may still be caught up in speedstress' momentum. "The moments where I was snuggling with my child and loving my child, I wasn't enjoying that the way that I feel like I should," recalls young mother, Rebecca, with regard to her speedstress. "It was more like, 'OK, this is what I need to do, this is duh duh duh duh duh, running through all the lists in my head…'"

Having become used to staying on the go, Rebecca had a hard time taking in her daughter's presence, not to mention experiencing a joyful response. Outer never fully met inner, and in that gap lay the measure of Rebecca's and her daughter's loss.

Jay Allison, a radio producer, finds that even interviews with strangers benefit from the powers of a slower pace. "To really sit and really look at someone and really probe and say, 'What about that?' and want the details … What astonishes me is the quality of interaction I have with people … when I'm talking to them in that way, and more particularly when I'm listening to them in that way."

Indeed, many of our relational gifts – whether listening, being intimate or seeking solace from a higher power – require slower rhythms. Our rushed and anxious thinking would have us believe that slowing down will cost us, but it turns out that quite the opposite is true.

Slowing down allows us to become more attuned to our internal experience, to recognizing what *is*, whether a physical need, a feeling, or a whisper of an old dream. As you regularly take the time to respond kindly to yourself – even if for only a few seconds – you'll find that your eyes will open more to others' needs and delights. Nourished, you'll nourish loved ones more. As painter Marcy Litle puts it, "The time that it takes to be as present as you can be is not taking away but is actually adding. It's like switching from doing to being and then trying to figure out how doing can emerge from being."

Reader, slowing down asks us not to be selfish, but to be self-ish. The "ish" like a mirror reflecting back a respect for what's real and true for you. We can't be self-ish all the time, of course, but we can do it far more than is usual when we're speedstressed.

Shelley Beason chose to be self-ish as she moved into retirement from her job in healthcare. Realizing that she needed greater balance in her life, Shelley intentionally didn't commit much of her newly free time. As a result, she had more of herself to give. "My primary relationship with my husband is infinitely better," Shelley says. "He says that I am a much more pleasant person to be around. I'm much more relaxed. I am more flexible, just sort of easier going."

Shelley's husband would not only know this, he would sense it. In fact, it's research-proven that the way you feel influences others. Specific types of neurons in our brains mirror the signs and expressions of others' emotional experience. Your bright eyes and upturned lips will bring a smile to my face, while my tears will elicit sadness in you. Mirror neurons likely play a role in making stress contagious; we've all had the experience of feeling jumpy after spending time with someone who is very "revved up."

As you move toward being more self-ish, remember that your frown, your gesture of impatience or annoyed tone of voice, do not belong to you alone, they migrate into others' experiences. In fact, we are so sensitive to each other that our first impressions are formed within seconds.

Because our anxious pace feeds our stress, and our stressed reactions flash, quite literally, into others' brains, slowing down is far from selfish. Slowing to kindly take in, and attend to, your own experience will prove a gateway to attending to others', as Dominique Davis discovered when she began "consciously" watching her own pace and energy expenditure. "If we don't slow down and we don't take time to rest ourselves and to delight ourselves, whatever slowing down [is] for us in any moment, how do we have empathy for other people?" she asks.

Sadly, we often don't when we're speedstressed. So, be self-ish: Cultivate an awareness of what you need, then plant the seeds for it. What you harvest will not be yours alone.

What's my slowlution?

≋ Notice the difference in your mood and behavior when you forgo needed rest or fun. Then, notice how you change after allowing yourself such care. Do you interact differently with others?

≋ Spend time with someone you know to be rushed and anxious. Then, do the same with someone who has a calmer pace. As you do, notice what effect each person has on you.

Chapter 8

Help Yourself, Help Your Employer

*"Slowing down means that one experiences more
and there's a greater understanding of the greater impact
of small events – and that includes the value of a dollar."*

~ John Abodeely

No organization sets out to encourage the development of chronic haste and anxiety in its employees. Yet it happens all too often. "I remember having lunch conversations with colleagues and them saying 'I'm exhausted. I don't know how much more I can do and I understand we're going to get another project and I can barely keep up now'," recalls Stelle Shumann of her experience at large corporations.

As Stelle's comment makes clear, speedstress often leaves workers feeling tired and demoralized The constant pressure to do more is also highly invalidating because it turns a blind eye to employees' wider lives and their essential need for balance. In this chapter, we'll explore why slowing down can prove a boon to your on-the-job performance; in a later chapter, we'll look at ideas for how to do so briefly and discretely in the workplace.

The institutional pressures that drive speedstress are varied: competition, lean staffing due to layoffs, and uncreative or outdated practices. And, of course, there are far too many enterprises that define success solely as growth at any cost in order to increase the bottom line. In the case of many non-profits, a limited budget stretched to meet bottomless customer needs ends up stretching employees too thin.

Ask any manager in a harried organization if a lack of care for its computing hardware and other equipment would be productive, and you'd likely hear a resounding No! The same can – and should – be said about employees. And yet, it too frequently is not. A recent study by the APA's Center for Organizational Excellence revealed that only 51 percent of respondents reported feeling appreciated on the job, with an equivalent bare majority stating that their employers valued work-life balance. Over a third of respondents reported regularly feeling stressed out at work, while a much greater proportion believed that on-the-job resources for stress management were insufficient.

Joe Colopy, founder and CEO of Bronto Software, is well aware of the dangers of not attending to employee well-being. "If people are being bled dry on a short-term basis … If someone works really hard and they can't self-manage that, or it's too much, and then they leave the company it's massively unproductive," says Colopy. He knows of what he speaks: Bronto has won numerous customer service and "best place to work "awards.

Speedstressed organizations are fundamentally flawed because what's not good for their employees is not good for them. "Productivity, as well as accuracy – or the lack thereof – is, over time, the more noticeable impact [of] stress," says John Mallard, the retired president of Cardinal State Bank.

How could this not be so? People – those who interact with customers, who strategize and create, and manage the technology – form the vital core of any enterprise. Unlike machinery, people have needs. Over time, if too many employees begin to feel exhausted, their lack of energy will prove a fault-line that sends tremors through the center of their organization.

We can't overlook the fact workers sometimes push themselves as hard, if not harder, than employers do. For Rebecca, who has worked in many a non-profit, believing in "the mission" made her and others susceptible to over-doing. "People seem[ed] to feel very driven," she recalls. "I found that there tends to be a lot of 'Let me show you how hard I can work.' You know, 'I'll work a little bit later. I'll work on the weekends.'"

Help yourself, help your employer

Do your workplace a favor: Revalue yourself. Begin to believe that you offer far more than the ability to scramble, and that your slower-paced abilities can save you time and help you work smarter. Revalue yourself because no computer, no machine, can offer all that you do. Only you and your colleagues can innovate, soothe a ruffled customer, or offer wise counsel. Only you can transmit the spirit that fires an enterprise up – or lays it low. Give yourself permission to slow down discreetly and in brief increments that do not jeopardize your employment.

Healing speedstress calls for you to be wiser than your speedstressed higher-ups. They may think that more work, done faster, has an unvarying positive correlation with more product and profit or, at the least, with their own job security. As we'll see, stress hinders productivity. We have only to call on reality to know this. Being speedstressed feels lousy, and rushing typically expends extra energy while making only the littlest dent in over-all workload. In addition, common sense tells us – and research bears out – that stress in the workplace lowers morale. As morale slides toward the negative, so do interactions between front-line employees and customers or clients. We've all experienced this. "When you go into a place," notes novelist Zelda Lockhart, "people are like 'Hey, you either buy it or you leave. I don't care. I don't have to be sweet to you.'" Too often, customers leave these transactions feeling bruised rather than valued. "What is that?," wonders Zelda.

"That" likely reflects the fact that nearly 40 percent of workers who feel highly overworked report feeling very angry with their employers, diminishing their internal motivation to provide helpful and friendly service. As a result, customer satisfaction, a driver of business' financial performance, suffers.

Stress has an even more potent effect on absences from work. According to ComPsych Corporation's StressPulse 2012 survey, more than half of respondents reported missing 1 to 2 days of work per year due to stress. Employee morale, customer service and productivity suffer when workers don't make it in.

Absenteeism is a shadowy foretelling of an even more costly fall-out: Employees quitting, as Joe Colopy indicated. In a 2007/2008 Global Strategic Rewards study of more than 900 companies worldwide, 37 percent of employees cited stress as their reason for resigning from a job. My pace-of-life survey is illustrative of how often people's minds turn to finding new work when they feel too rushed: Nearly half the responses to an open-ended question about how one could slow down were of the "Quit my job … Change my job … Find a job I like" variety.

Turnover costs are significant financial drains to organizations, ranging from half to three times or more the departed employee's salary. Indirect costs, such as errors made by the inexperienced new hire, as well as lowered morale and productivity in the previous worker's colleagues, also take a toll. Needless to say, in any industry, mid-level managers and top executives would cost far more to replace.

When a long-serving employee leaves, vast amounts of organizational knowledge, as well as established relationships with clients or customers, walk out the door. This is but one of many reasons to value yourself, even if your employers don't demonstrate the same inclination. Learning to regularly slow down from speedstress so that you can sustain a productive work life is a gift to both you and your employer. Below, we'll look in greater depth at reasons to cultivate more balance in your workday.

Successful relationship-building

Long before deals were closed on golf courses, traders and merchants sauntered harbor-side in medieval Venice, Hormuz and Singapore, gossiping and haggling over vats of wine, oils and exotic goods. Goodwill has driven commerce and other enterprises over the centuries. Our human relationships in the workplace – whether with co-workers, peers, customers, or suppliers - form a web that either supports individual efforts and organizational missions - or works against them.

Effective relationships are those built on what the psychologist Daniel Goleman has termed "emotional intelligence." This type of "know how" encompasses an awareness of one's own emotional responses, as well as an ability to manage them appropriately. The recognition of, and skillful response to, others' concerns also play a vital role. In the workplace, managers who are emotionally savvy understand that each employee is far more than the role they play at work, and that each has a deep need to be listened to, respected and encouraged.

Doing so demands that supervisors have the ability to slow down and attend to what's real for those reporting to them. Such management takes time, yet, supervisors who are able to convey their recognition of others' realities, even if they can't fully accommodate them, elicit loyalty and best efforts. Such workplaces foster morale and cooperation, rather than fear and intra-office rivalries. In an atmosphere of safety, workers are more likely to conceive – and offer - the risky, but creative, suggestions that can lead to innovation and promote success.

No matter one's rank in the workplace, slowing down in order to regain a greater sense of calm and self-control will contribute to the same in your workplace. (In fact, a U.S. general who suddenly found himself in an unorthodox work setting, discovered calm's power. Held hostage by guerrillas, the general believes that his intentional self-calming helped lessen his captors' emotional activation, making them less trigger-happy.)

Anxiety and stress, on the other hand, invite impatience, irritation, and judgment, distancing us from others. Psychotherapist Sharon Dornberg-Lee, whose work rises and falls on the strength of relationships, is not immune to such effects. As she sits with clients on hectic days, says Sharon, "I'll notice that I either feel less empathically present with clients or literally that I will be thinking about [unrelated things]. I'm also, I think, less tolerant … about clients' anxiety if I'm anxious myself, maybe more distancing from their anxiety."

When we are grumpy and rushed, it becomes easy, no matter one's work role or position, to overlook the importance of building and sustaining work relationships. Slowing down to, as pharmaceuticals executive Mary Bennett puts it, "find out what someone's up to in life" forges allies for turbulent times in the workplace. Yet, in speedstressed environments, taking a moment to inquire about a co-worker's home life or to toss around ideas for another's project can feel like an impediment to one's progress. Consequently, in such settings, cooperation and goodwill often take a back seat to getting the work done, with little or no credit given to how inter-connected they are.

Working in a "collaborative" manner is a must, says Kevin Webb, whose previous workplace solved industrial design problems. "I don't think you can do any sort of creative process or process of building anything in isolation and do it very effectively or have the energy to sustain it for later on," he told me. "If you're doing things that are hard, you definitely don't want to be doing it alone."

Speed of work and time on task

Scientists do strange things in pursuit of knowledge, including playing tricks on bees. In one experiment, researchers created a Plexiglas screen with small holes in it and, projecting colored circles around the holes, fashioned a "meadow" abloom. Only one of the colors, blue, surrounded holes offering a drop of sucrose; the other colors circled water-filled holes. How, the scientists wondered, would bees moving at differing speeds do in accurately selecting the bounty of the blue?

Scientists have conducted similar experiments with people. As it turns out, the results are similar across bees and humans: As one makes choices, or discriminates, more quickly, the tendency to make errors rises. In humans, this effect has earned its own moniker: "the speed-accuracy trade-off." The effect applies across a wide range of tasks, from proofreading to security. In a research-driven simulation of airport security screening, an emphasis on speed resulted in a decline in the recognition of target objects.

The speed-accuracy trade-off alone casts significant doubt on the logic that rushing will result in moving through more tasks - period. Errors cost us far more than the time needed to rectify them. Speed-related errors can sully reputations, cost organizations money, and create misinformation that hinders desired outcomes.

Researchers have also identified another effect relevant to speedstress: the longer our time on task, the greater our mental fatigue. Arousal and motivation decline and, like it or not, attention inadvertently flags, causing an unplanned "break" from work. A slip in attention – whether during the coding of an element of a computerized algorithm or the stacking of a heavy highway load - can have far reaching impacts.

Give yourself – and the quality of your work – a similar break. In order to work most effectively, slow down as you need to.

Effective problem-solving

In 1925 physicist Werner Heisenberg had a bad case of hay fever in Munich, Germany. His affliction was no doubt made worse by fretful hours spent laboring over a scientific obstacle to the development of what is now called quantum physics. Heisenberg, seeking relief from his allergy, took himself for 10 days to an archipelago in the North Sea called Heligoland. Heligoland's red cliffs, set against sparkling blue sea, offered stunning scenery, as well as pollen-free air. The island's peace and isolation meant rest and "having good time to think over the questions," as Heisenberg described in an interview years later.

In his guesthouse near the ocean late one night, Heisenberg's unpressured thinking paid off in the needed breakthrough. His willingness to slow down had opened the door for quantum physics far wider.

The physicist's vacation demonstrates the importance of stress reduction to problem-solving. Research shows us that the more positive our mood, the more quickly we find solutions. With Heisenberg, we began at the end of a problem-solving process; however, as soon as a problem is identified, any cultivation of calm energy will prove of value. Carefully defining the full nature of a problem, rather than anxiously rushing to fix it, is essential to devising an effective solution. Indeed, experts on human survival tell us that a panicked reaction to trouble in the wild, for example, invites disaster, while a cool-headed analysis of changing conditions can point one toward a positive outcome.

"Whenever you have a problem you have to put it down in words - what it is you're going to do," says Kevin Webb. "I think that's the hardest part because it takes a lot of effort to do that well, but I think it's also about slowness."

Having practiced *i slow* with cursors blinking and tasks still undone, you will be more likely to promote, as Kevin puts it, "stepping back ... and saying 'O.K., what is the actual situation?'" Clear problem-definition leads to sensible prioritization and the appropriate matching of resources to the problem at hand. Yet, deliberate problem-solving in the workplace also requires the application of a critical eye to your solution, notes Kevin. "You have to say 'I've done this. I've figured out something about it and now I need to step away from it and look at it again.' I think it connects to the idea of slowness in a big way. You can't just try to cut corners and save time by continuing to push things in a certain direction."

Each potential solution needs to be assessed for its negative and positive impacts on the organization, as well as on clients and customers. For instance, environmental, political, or image issues may come into play. How well does the fix fit with an organization's mission? What hidden costs could arise unexpectedly? Be the person who calmly remembers that the investigation of such queries before solutions are put into place can save money in the long-term.

Risk and mastery

Changing a speedstress habit involves risk: For example, that of not following through with our resolution to change and, therefore, disappointing ourselves; or, the perceived risk of not employing one's customary pace on the job. Consequently, the practice of slowing down can help you become more comfortable with tolerating risk. Learning to do so wisely can be crucial to progressing in the workplace, as well as to offering more to your employer.

Potentially beneficial risks are those that, whether sought-out or assigned, will help you advance in your career if you successfully meet them. These can include taking the initiative to define new opportunities and, then, rising to them. For instance, an employee might suggest a new twist for a longstanding process, or map out reasons for venturing into an unfamiliar market. Assigned positive risk - for example, being tapped to give a last-minute presentation - also provides a chance to stand out. At the moment you're selected, however, you may feel like a tiger has been thrown into your lap. Here, your regular practice of the *s-step's* scan will help you more promptly recognize internal tension that might provoke an unproductive reaction (*You want me to do what?!!*).

Slowing down from stress can also play a positive role in lessening occupational risks. We see this no more clearly than with sleep. A worker who makes a practice of getting adequate sleep will bring a fresher mind, sharper memory and greater ability to concentrate to the workplace, while the sleep-deprived will be more prone to making mistakes. A Harvard Medical School study in 2012 identified insomnia as the likely culprit in 274,000 accidents and mistakes on the job, ratcheting up costs by $31 billion.

Speedstressed practices – from rushing through tasks to not listening carefully – inject a level of risk that has the potential to cost organizations not merely dollars, but lives and reputations. Sarah, formerly a hospital midwife, wrote me that she began to practice home birth because the schedule imposed on her by the hospital meant, "I was constantly having to make decisions about whether to spend the time needed or stay on schedule."

When a midwife – or any worker - gives up "time needed," the process in need of that time becomes subject to risk. (In fact, these pressures caused enough stress to Sarah that she resigned her post.) Cautiously navigating your own needs and those of your job so as to manage risk will keep you out of a rogue's gallery of employees. Such workers, says Mary Bennett, "are so hyper all the time that, literally, they'll make decisions or do things that I'll think to myself, 'Have you not thought through the consequences of that?'"

Reflection, Enjoyment & Creativity

As we've seen, positive emotions increase our ability to open our minds. In fact, researchers recommend doing something you enjoy before addressing a creative challenge. The ability to relax, letting the mind wander, is central to this process. Yet, such free-form thought is often not highly valued at work. "One element that's often missing is a lack of reflection," says John Abodeely. "It doesn't appear productive, it's a long-term investment … often eschewed for short-term productivity." John should know as his career has included introducing creativity and the arts into many American institutions.

Steve Muth, inventor of both a toy and a website, has a strong appreciation of reflection's rewards. Without taking the time to let his mind roam, he says, "I'm never going to figure out anything new or anything difficult. You've got to have the time that's truly free. You're not in a rush. As I dig down, to say 'I'm not sure where I'm going to end up.' Instead, being in a state of wonder…you have to wonder about something."

A 2005 McKinsey study of more than 100 manufacturing companies concluded that those with the best financial results were encouraging innovative work processes instead of increasing workloads. At Apple Computer, home to lifestyle-altering creations, innovation meant that no decision about the shape, size or function of products could be rushed through. Steve Jobs made repeated visits to Apple's design room, where he simply handled the product prototypes, silently taking in their look and feel as he pondered their fit with customers' lives. Many creative conversations with the top designer flowed from those visits. "Some of the better ideas do come to you at odd hours in different places," says Bob Thomas, former CEO of Charles & Colvard. "You hear stories about people keeping the pad next to the bed. It's about being aware without being aware. Our minds operate on a lot of different levels."

Thomas was often grateful that many of his managers worked in Hong Kong, as their emails would arrive as he was going to bed. According to Thomas, the time difference provided "time to reflect and think about whatever the issues might be and about what a good strategy might be."

So, take your own reflective ramble; make it a slowlution. Lean back in your chair, close your eyes and think of nothing but new angles for a process or a creative pitch. Relax; enjoy this productive pursuit.

Productivity

In between gigs, rock musician Keith Spring often made a point of visiting his longtime music teacher in Louisville. During one get-together, the teacher told Keith that he had stopped to chat one day with a drummer who taught lessons through a local music store. Keith continues the story: "The drummer told my teacher, he said 'Yeah, I've got over a hundred students every week now taking private lessons.' And my teacher said, 'You know what? You may have a hundred students, but you're not teaching a hundred people'."

Keith laughed; he knew what his teacher meant. The drummer's reasoning inferred that more was better. "He's making more money, he's getting more students and he's efficient," notes Keith. "In his mind he's teaching all these people, but I don't think it works that way. That hasn't been my experience." To Keith, the drummer reflected contemporary business' narrow definition of productivity.

If we consider productivity as simply the ratio of inputs to outputs (for instance, employee hours to quantity of product) – then working ever faster takes on a seductive sheen. Yet, many studies exist in which employees attribute lowered productivity to stress on the job. According to ComPsych Corporation's 2012 study, 41 percent of employees reported losing 15 to 30 minutes per day of productivity, while a 2009 survey stated that 51 percent of workers said stress affected their output.

Little surprise here. Speed's role in productivity must still be balanced against human needs, as we've seen, and the quality of the end-product. What's the use of putting out more and more widgets if they arrive flawed at your customer's door? Of working so fast that you never notice the major error in your report? As inventor Steve Muth told me, today's pressure to do more with fewer resources results in "getting by, by doing a lot…and it's going to be mediocre."

It is exactly at the juncture of productivity and quality that slowing down will help you shine. Quality demands smarts, and smarts demands regular de-stressing. Bronto CEO Joe Colopy agrees with this. The most efficient maximization of profit rests on the maximization of any enterprise's most valued resource, its employees. "Sometimes you need to push people and you need to motivate them," notes Colopy, "and other times you need to say 'Listen, you need to go home and just relax.' You actually get more productivity out of a person by not burning them out. You need to find the right balance and for everyone that's different."

Alternating focused work time with *i slow* practices allows you to investigate and support your own balance (Now, can you have the exact balance you need or want during work hours? Of course not; but you can move closer to it.) You'll also have a better chance of standing out - not as the person who got it done fast, but as the one who got it done better. Choose to be the person who is deliberate enough to spot flaws before they are mass-produced; who is rested and calm enough to come up with the idea that brings in new customers.

Noticing the details

A tiny shop in my town regularly takes note of its customers' impromptu and witty expressions of delight. Instead of allow-ing the remarks to trail into the air as the shoppers leave, the employees tout them in colorful script on a two-sided whiteboard outside the front door.

Listening for and recording such comments is a detail many retail establishments might consider too insubstantial to under-take. Certainly, preparing the sign is but a tiny sliver of the work that goes on in the store, and the whiteboard itself is far smaller than the size you'd hang in your home office. Yet, even after passing the store scores, if not hundreds, of times over the years,

I am always drawn to the sign's clever remarks. And, oftentimes, its reminder of the shop's unique offerings lures me in for an unintended visit.

Success often rises and falls on such details. Often, though, speedstressed employees are too rushed to notice and too stressed to care. Let slowing down change that. Your worth as an employee will expand if you take time to identify opportunities for improvement and innovation. Perhaps a seat cushion is loose in the waiting room, or your employer's zip code is incorrect on its invoice forms. Ask yourself, *How might this affect customers…our sales…our mission?*

Higher-ups with an eye on quality will note not only your powers of observation, but also the fact that you care.

What's my slowlution?

⪉ Select two insights from this chapter to use as motivation to slow down into greater effectiveness on the job. How do you want to implement them?

⪉ How has being speedstressed had a negative impact on your work product or on your standing as an employee? (Inquire kindly!)

Into the Garden

Preparing to Slow Down

Chapter 9

Enriching the Soil:
Valuing your Onelife

"Everything rests on the tip of motivation."

~ Claudia Horwitz

*"Ask some questions about identifying what it is you want in your life:
Is it possible, and are you willing to make it possible?
And then, let go and trust you'll find [the] way."*

~ Dominique Davis

How do you want to value your patch of time on this earth? Often we lose touch with both the question and the answer when we are speedstressed. Yet, our response often offers us powerful motivation for slowing down.

In posing the question, I use the verb "value" in its most active sense: the intentional sculpting of choices that simultaneously reflect who we are and enrich us as we move forward from one moment into the next. Evidence of such valuing can be found in the choice of Nelson Mandela and his fellow inmates to grow new life while confined to prison on Robben Island, a rocky, wave-pounded site of such barren harshness that even the guards referred to it as "blue hell."

Mr. Mandela and other prisoners dug a small garden plot against a wall in the prison yard. There, Mr. Mandela nurtured a single tomato plant. The plant responded with red and tender bounty, as Mr. Mandela reported in an exhibit of drawings and commentary entitled "Spirit of Freedom." Sadly, despite Mr. Mandela's best efforts, the tomato plant eventually died. So attached was Mr. Mandela to the plant that he rinsed its lifeless roots off before gently covering it with soil.

Cultivation – whether of plant-life or new behaviors – is never easy, which makes identifying why we want to slow down all the more important. Motivation will see you through the anxiety of *not* resorting to a hasty pace; it will help you persist in the face of distractions and diversions, and there will be many: Your to-do list will not suddenly shrink, and, while others may not consciously recognize that your pace has altered, they will sense a change. "[If] I'm not working as I've always worked," says leadership coach Joan Roberts Eastman, "then other people around me are going to think, 'What's going on? She's different.' … They may actually try to shift me back."

As fatigue and tension wrap through us like the confining walls of a prison, they can cut us off from our deepest sense of worth or purpose. They can sever us from our essential human drive to actively value our life by engaging more zestfully or deeply with it. As a result, deep unanswered hungers - whether to notice *here* and *now* more, to germinate a special talent, or to love more openly - often arise, adding to our stress.

With his gentle movements and provision of care, Mr. Mandela surely nourished a part of himself that prison had starved: the need to believe in life's potential for tenderness and bounty. His coaxing of green shoots from dusty earth must have offered our gardener reassurance that life was something to value, that he had not lost touch with its gentler side.

73

Pay attention, as those prisoners did, to what tugs at you. You'll find useful information there about how you want to live your life. A few years back, when slow-time was deficient in my life, I began to notice that when I walked across my front porch toward my car, I would frequently experience a distinct desire to veer sideways toward a comfortable chair by the porch railing. I didn't anticipate this experience, yet it happened repeatedly and it told me a lot, offering me further motivation to slow down.

Kindly notice your recurring inner tugs, thoughts, or inclinations; they're not right or wrong, they simply are. Some part of you is in need of your attention, is trying to tell you that something's missing, that change is necessary. Respond kindly to your inner messenger; it's your ally. When slowing down seems impossible and you question why you're making the effort, you can lean on its essential message: That haste and stress can pull us away, moment by moment, from cultivating the life we truly want.

As you respond, it may help to picture yourself as a gardener, with the word "one" perched in your palm like a bulb you are about to press deep into life's rich soil: *One*life. Say it to yourself. Then, ask,

Your seed: i slow

i	**intentionally**	and regularly (4 times/day):
s	**say**	"I slow" as you take a slow, deep breath
	stop or **slow** **scan**	your *pace* your *energy level* & *tension*
l	**listen**	for the answer to *What's my slowlution?*
o	**opt**	to enter into your slowlution, for 30 seconds or more, with as much <u>focus</u> as is safely possible.
w	**watch**	actively for reward(s).

Does speedstress allow me to live as if I truly value my onelife? If the answer is *No*, resolve again to cultivate a new pace, using *i slow* as your seed practice.

In the early stages, your efforts to slow down will not be so different from Mr. Mandela's. He acted on his intention (*i-step*), asking the warden for permission to plant the garden and to tend it day by day. Each time he arrived at the patch of green, he surely slowed down to scan its state (*s-step*) and listened to what the scan revealed (*l-step*) – perhaps, a need for weeding or watering – before opting to provide the care (*o-step*). You can likely imagine, as I do, that the famous prisoner bent to his work with great focus.

Recounting the loss of the tomato plant in later years, Mr. Mandela made clear that he had been observant of the rewards (*w-step*) he gained from its tending. He wrote that his grief had helped him develop a greater appreciation for the importance of fostering loving relationships.

Meditation served as Claudia Horwitz's seed practice after the migraines and irritability of "burn out" caused her to question her life. "I'd sit for 10 or 15 minutes, it wasn't very long but it was enough to really start transforming my life in these mysterious ways …", says Claudia. "The act of doing it every day was such an honoring of some other form of wisdom, some quieter part of myself."

As your practice infuses your life with respect and kindness, you'll want more. You'll also experience the reality that slow's greatest reward lies not in any slowlution, but in regularly returning your awareness from tasks in order to recognize and respond to what's true for you. Luckily, your cultivation of change doesn't rest on the permission of an external authority, as Mr. Mandela's garden did. It does require, however, that you have some motivating answers ready in moments of discouragement or struggle, as Dominique Davis came to understand.

The young woman was renovating a house at the same time she was in the process of restoring herself through slowing down. As Dominique became more aware of her speedstressed habits, her inner struggle at lunchtime became increasingly evident. She noticed that, even when hunger pangs interfered with keeping an effective focus on painting, she still felt driven "to plow through, work all day, until like blood's coming out of the skin. I hate breaking for lunch, I hate to do it … it's like, 'No, you don't need that'."

Having identified the speedstressed "abrasiveness" with which she treated herself, Dominique decided to interrupt the pattern. When hunger called with walls still unpainted, Dominique challenged herself to become clear on what she most valued in her in life: "Is it working through and getting this trim done in another hour," she asked, "or is it eating a meal and saying grace for it, and giving thanks for just being alive?"

In an age in which there will always be more "trim" to complete, let your questions and your answers bend you toward your desired pace of life, eager as Mr. Mandela in that prison garden.

What's my slowlution?

- ⮑ Think of the deepest desire you have for your life, and how changing your pace might help you coax it into reality over time. If you can't identify such a desire, have faith that slowing down will help you recognize it.

- ⮑ Gently inquire: *Does speedstress allow me to live as if I truly value my onelife?* If the answer is *No*, divert from any self-judgment. Instead, focus on what actively valuing your life would look like. What small changes could you make now?

Chapter 10

Tilling: Turning Motivation to Decision

"I was becoming somebody ... that I did not want to become and I did not recognize ... and I was like 'Enough'."

~April Yvonne Garrett

As she began slowing down, Kerry Johnson began to intentionally wander down the hill from her house to visit her goats. She spent time watching their relaxed alertness. "It's kind of contagious when you hang out with them. They make me laugh," she says.

The goats' light, playful manner helped Kerry to connect with her motivations for slowing her life down. Her story also teaches us that unexpected or offbeat experiences can inform us as we move toward change. So, remain open to what strikes you as you define your most compelling reasons for regularly easing back from stress and hurry.

We can think of motivation as the mental and emotional energy fueling not only a decision to change, but the act of doing so. In this chapter, we'll explore tools for kindling that energy in you.

Cultivating motivation

Look back

Look back to the moment when you reached out your hand to pick up this book. What fact or feeling prompted you to do so? What words went through your mind? If you struggled with making the purchase or checking the book out, what caused you to follow through with it?

> **?**
>
> **What is my whole life telling me about my speedstressed pace?**

You might also want to get out a photo of yourself as a child in a moment of play or pleasure. Put it in a prominent place. Look back to that time, and believe that you deserve to feel that way more often as an adult. You do! We never outgrow our need for rest and recreation.

Inventory speedstress' costs

Begin actively – and kindly - looking for all the changes and costs wrought by your pace. Ask yourself: *What is my whole life telling me about my speedstressed pace?* For instance, explore whether get-togethers with friends, which you used to look forward to, now feel like impediments to getting things done? Are you staying later and later at the office? Are you keeping busy in retirement because you want to - or because you want to impress others? Is there increased conflict in your primary relationship because you're distracted and hurried?

Your body is as honest a source of information as you'll ever find. Let it help shift your motivation into a decision to change. *What do you observe and feel in your body?* Notice how you feel when you wake up in the morning. At other times of the day, what is your body telling you about speedstress' impact?

For instance, if you sigh every time you hurry across your front porch to your car, wonder why. The *s-step* will help immensely in recognizing these speedstressed costs.

Tension, elevated blood pressure, decreased sexual desire and many other physiological symptoms can serve as powerful motivators. Pay attention to your moods, your overall enjoyment of life. What are they telling you?

Interview others

Interview loved ones for feedback about the effect your current pace of life is having on you and, possibly, on them. (Remember, practice kindness to self if you feel upset by what you hear. You are working on change for the better!) Encourage friends and family to be specific about everything from physical changes, to your mood, to what you say about your own life. What's their impression of how your pace affects your relationship with them, of how well you listen? Often others notice speedstress' impact earlier than we can. Let the distance between "what *is*" and "what I truly *want*" become clearer.

Plumb your inner life

Your inner life may offer all manner of motivations, so pay attention. Our emotions, intuitions and dreams can yield information about what we truly want and need. Become aware of what pulls at you, what you long for; these can act as strong motivators. Kerry's review of her values also energized her change of pace. "I'd always thought you're supposed to earn as much as you can," recalled Kerry. She began to pay attention to her love of free time and creative pursuits; soon, she reassessed what she really needed, deciding "I don't need as much … Instead of working to earn a living, I want to live."

Harness your anger – skillfully!

Many people who are speedstressed seem irritated due to fatigue and sleeplessness, but beneath the surface, they are often angry - angry that their employers don't treat them respectfully, that technology runs ceaselessly, and tasks seem never to end. They – possibly, you - are resentful of a lack of time for hobbies, loved ones and, even, careful thought. Often anger is also a cover for a feeling of disempowerment with regards to doing anything besides staying on the run.

If you are aware of similar feelings, let yourself know that they are valid – and they require careful handling. Remind yourself that you aren't a victim: You are taking steps to change your pace. Let anger's hot energy re-fire your motivation to persist. If you find yourself having problems keeping your temper in check, seek out a mental health professional. All of us can benefit from extra support and input when we're very stressed.

Read gravestones

Caught up in speedstress, we fret about the scarcity of time for all we have to do, but we rarely consider how short our *one*life is for the living, or how tenuous. Begin to do so. When you feel ready, walk slowly through a cemetery.

Gravestones are pages chiseled with our shared stories. The people buried beneath them probably lay plans and dreams like shiny tracks across the decades they believed they'd have. Yet, the carved words in any cemetery make clear that life offers no guarantee beyond the present moment, and death cares not a bit about our future plans. These are perhaps the most powerful truths denied by speedstressed thinking. Acknowledging them can serve as powerful motivation to change.

Imagine

After years spent freeing herself from living according to "shoulds," Mariah Darlington regularly sinks into a rewarding slowlution for a few minutes. "I'll just sit in the quiet … It kind of clears my mind and things seem to fall into place in a better way."

Imagine now that you have been slowing down for the last year. You are as comfortable with the process as Mariah is, having practiced regularly. Now, zoom in, and imagine that you are in the middle of a slow-down (make it energizing or calming, according to your needs right now). Be specific. What time is it? Where would you be? Would you be alone? What would you be seeing, hearing, feeling? Let yourself drop as much as you can into the experience of both the slowlution and being comfortable with it.

When you're done, think about how your period of easing back might have benefitted the imagined "you." Or, perhaps your imagining actually did you some good in reality! How might the rewards ripple through your day? How might your life be different if you slowed down in that manner every day – even if very briefly - for a week, a month, a year?

Deciding

In order to transform your motivation into a decision for change, you'll need to decide that the following are true for you:

1. *You are in the habit of moving at a pace faster than you like on more days than you want.*

We can't intentionally transform what we don't accept as existing. "There are times when I feel like my life is ahead of me and I'm hurrying to catch up," says Melany Coopmans Vizithum.

"That means I keep not accepting how the day is." If we can accept not only our pace, but also the challenges of each day, then we can take steps in the present to work with them more effectively.

So, if you think it true, very kindly accept that speedstress has become an unhelpful influence in your life – and that you want to change. I emphasize using kindness because motivation thrives on it; conversely, nothing kills our drive to try new behaviors more quickly than self-judgment (think of pursuits you've dropped because you were critical of your abilities).

2. *The cost of speedstress now outweighs any rewards.*

As you accept the reality of your hasty way of life, take a good look at what it's costing you and, possibly, your loved ones. In fact, start a list and look at it every day. You may discover surprising effects (for example, perhaps your dental health has suffered because you hurry through brushing).

As you take note of these costs, be sure to practice kindness. To develop habits is human. Some are more helpful than others, but they all begin as a seemingly beneficial coping method. Our evolutionary drive toward survival wouldn't have it any other way! If you're like most people, you probably didn't notice when your coping ran away with your quality of life.

3. *Your dilemma's solution lies within.*

"Don't expect it to ever slow down around you," says Joan Roberts Eastman. "The way the world is going … You'll always have too much to do."

She's so right. The quantity of your demands is unlikely to change, nor is our speed-loving culture, so *you* must change, one small choice at a time. Take personal responsibility for reshaping your pace. If you've felt victimized by your demands, deciding to "own" yourself as the solution will feel empowering. It will also open your eyes to a reality speedstress often obscures: You are your own best resource. Thankfully, you are exactly what you can control.

What's my slowlution?

◌ Practice some of the exercises above. Write down your top two motivations for slowing down.

◌ What do your motivations suggest about how you might live out your decision to slow down? If, for example, health concerns are motivators, you might want to consider rest or exercise as your slow-down in the *o-step*.

Sowing the Seeds
of a Slower Pace

The Steps of "*i slow*"

Chapter 11

Intention is Everything: The *i-step*

Intentionally and regularly (4 times each day)
choose to take an 'i slow' break.

Sailors of ancient times interpreted the northeasterly winds that swept the Mediterranean as a signal of the gods' displeasure. Still, they set sail again and again, fueled by their intention to reach other shores. Centuries later and thousands of miles westward, early farmers on our country's plains were equally deliberate in the face of blizzard winds. Twice each stormy day, without fail, they left their fire-warmed shelters to tend to their livestock, grasping snow ropes strung between home and barn like corded maps of the wind-whipped terrain.

As you begin to slow down, take heart from these examples of resolute perseverance in the face of that most natural form of speedstress, wind. Set, and reset, your intention (*i-step*) to regularly practice all the steps of *i slow*. Without that first step, the others will blow away like snow ropes loosed from their moorings by the prevailing "winds" of habit, anxiety, and cultural pressure.

The five steps of *i slow* are designed, with repeated use, to help you let go of habitual haste. In order to change any accustomed behavior we need to regularly:

- be intentional about doing so (*i-step*),
- notice the habitual behavior pattern and its effect (*s-step*),
- substitute a new behavior (*l-* and *o-steps*), and
- watch actively for rewards from the new behavior (*w-step*), and
- record basic details of new behavior for the first few weeks, if possible.

As Claudia Horwitz grew her non-profit, Stone Circles, she realized she needed to take some downtime before she left for business trips. You can hear Claudia set her intention in this snippet of self-talk: "OK, I need a small window where I can taper my work off before I leave, instead of skidding into the airport."

With her intention clear, Claudia created the slower time she needed.

Habits, by their nature, like to hang on, so your best intentions for slowing down will run into internal resistance. Counterintuitive as it may seem to do, acknowledge the resistance and reframe it as a predictable part of change. After all, shifting old behaviors is often more hard work than fun: Who likes dealing with the temporary spike in anxiety that often occurs? Going fast may be draining and counter-productive, but its familiarity will, at first, feel easier than slowing down.

So, expect resistance. Accept its presence, and then refocus on fueling your intention to reshape your pace.

Strengthen your intention

Cue i slow

As you become more skilled at noticing your pace or tension, that recognition will begin to act as a natural trigger for slowing down. Until then, I encourage you to schedule in four *i slow* practices a day. As Marcy Litle learned, "The biggest thing [about slowing down] is to not forget the practices that keep me grounded even though they take time."

The i-step

INTENTIONALLY CHOOSE to take an *i slow* break 4 times each day.

Strengthen your intention:

- SCHEDULE in your *i slows.*

- CUE yourself to practice *i slow.*

- FIND THE ABSURDITY in not practicing.

- Form a SLOWING CIRCLE.

- RECORD your progress – make it real.

- Remind yourself of WHY

Reminders are often the vehicles that carry us daily from intention to practice. In addition to scheduling your slow-downs, post notes or related images prominently – whether on your bathroom mirror, computer, or desk – and change them up so you keep noticing them.

Research has found that the likelihood of a certain behavior happening can be strengthened by a person's unconscious awareness of relevant objects; for instance, a briefcase can "prime" people to become more competitive. Use this to your advantage, sprinkling symbols of "things slow" in the areas you inhabit most. A photo of yourself twirling a basketball, a dish of sand from a favorite beach, or the sound of soothing music might serve to prime your practice of *i slow.*

Recurring events can serve as both reminders and opportunities for slowing down. Those might include eating (chew slowly, taking in tastes and sensations), walking the dog (slowly, with focus on your feet meeting the pavement), or waiting on line (slow focused breathing, or visualization).

Find the absurdity

"When I was working full-time and struggling to find time to exercise," Sarah writes, "… I'd make myself say out loud, 'Doing the laundry is more important to me right now than taking care of myself.' That's almost always so absurd that it would help me get a grip on my priorities."

Shore up your intention by presenting yourself with similar exaggerations, as in: *I don't deserve 25 minutes of self-care out of 1,020 waking minutes a day …* Or, *Slowing down for five minutes will make everything go to pieces for hours.* Say these out loud; take in their absurdity. Then, practice.

Prioritize yourself

The quality and intensity of your actions and communications are seamlessly influenced by *how you are.* When Joan Roberts Eastman puts a task aside, she reminds herself, "My priority at this moment is to take care of myself, so I can do the task better later."

You can't bring your best self to your work or to your loved ones if you're not at your best. Now, can you be at your best all – or, even, most - of the time? Of course not! But, slowing down can help you move toward calmer energy.

Form a "slowing circle"

Keep an eye out for others you know and like who want to lessen their stress and hurry. Invite them to join you in updating the sewing circles that surely drew some of your female ancestors together: Form a *slowing circle*.

When cultural tides pull you away from slowing down, circle members can remind you of your intention, as well as provide natural rewards such as humor, encouragement, and good ideas. Circle members can also act as kind monitors for each other, checking in weekly or daily as to whether members are practicing *i slow* on a regular basis. Their disappointment when you have been carried off by speed again, paired with brainstorming about how you might respond differently in the upcoming week, can prove helpfully reinforcing.

Whether your circle is large or small, whether it's "virtual" or in-person, matter little as long as you feel "joined" in your efforts to live at a pace that nurtures your quality of life. Claudia Horwitz reached out to others as she struggled to find a way to ease her fatigue and pattern of overwork. "I wanted to feel held in the process," recalls Claudia. "I do think it's powerful to have communities of people supporting each other to make particular decisions."

After feeling isolated by your demands, a slowing circle can be a wonderful place to grow new friendships, as well as a new pace of life. (For a free supplement on slowing circles, please visit www.slowlutions.com.)

Make your efforts real

Early on in habit change, a regularly weekly review of your progress (whether on your own or with slowing circle members) can spur you to act on your intention. I recommend creating a very simple form that you fill in after each *i slow* (see example on page 92). Doing so will not only signal intentionality - *I'm serious about this* - it will provide you valuable information about shifting patterns in your pace, energy level, and tension. If you're in a slowing circle, select an on-line site where you and your comrades can share the information.

Decide ahead of time how many completed *i slows* per day will constitute success for you (I recommend 4, but start with 3 if more is impractical for you.) Over the first few weeks of practice, you'll be able to spot associations between specific slowlutions and rewards.

If you are avoiding slowing down, as you may well, these forms will provide stark evidence, providing you the chance to renew your intention. With enough sheets completed, their abundance will serve as reinforcing evidence of your commitment, efforts, and progress.

What's my slowlution?

≋ Plan two ways to strengthen your intention to practice. For example, you might want to tie the thought *"Today, I will slow down by* [specific slowlution]" to the act of pouring your first cup of coffee. Or, set your smart-phone timer for *i slow* breaks.

≋ Think about whom you might ask to join a slowing circle. Would the circle meet in person or have "virtual" interactions? Imagine!

≋ Create a sample recording form to be filled out after each practice for a few weeks, or copy the one on the next page. (When choosing rating levels, go with the number between 1 and 7 that first comes into your mind.)

Date: _____.   *i slow* #: _____.

My *s-step* scan revealed: _____.

_____.

_____.

Pace of movement/activity **just before** *i slow*: _____.
1 - 7 (1 = extremely slow... 7 = extremely fast)

Tension: _____.   1 - 7 (1 = extremely calm... 7 = extremely tense)

Energy level: _____. 1 - 7 (1 = extremely energized... 7 = extremely tired)

Slowlution(s) used: _____.

_____.

_____.

Reward(s): _____.

_____.

_____.

Form not available at times? Memorize the categories:
P, T, E (1-7), Sl, R.

Chapter 12

Slow, Scan, Listen:
The *s-* and *l-steps*

"Becoming aware of my breath, scanning my body, feeling my feet on the Earth ... remembering to be conscious of the present moment."

~ Sarah's scan

When we live too much on the run, even the most basic information about our pace and bodily experience can become lost to us. "I'd get in the car to go to work and I would think, 'I have no idea what I'm wearing, no idea what I have on my face. I have no idea if I've eaten breakfast. I've had no thought about myself at all'," Rebecca recalls.

No thought about myself at all.

The s-step

say	"I slow" as you take a slow, deep breath
slow or **stop**	your pace
scan	your energy level & tension

Rebecca's experience highlights how focusing on the next task, and the next, at a quick pace can cause us to regularly lose touch with our in-the-moment awareness of our experience in mind, body and feelings. As a result, we repeatedly bypass our needs and desires. We also remain unaware of how automatic unhelpful behaviors have become. Now, can we be fully aware of our self all of the time? Of course not, and neither would that be appropriate. However, we can try to invite a more balanced awareness so that our level of self-care is healthful and helpful.

The s-step

In the *s-step*, you will circle your attention back from tasks *out there* to your reality *in here*. As you interrupt your hasty pace to scan, think of yourself as a gardener in early spring, kneeling by the edge of your still unsown soil, eyeing it, rubbing it between your fingers, assessing what it needs.

As you begin this step, say "I slow," out loud or silently, and take a slow deep breath. Let your inhalation and exhalation act like a brake, slowing your pace of movement or activity (stopping it, ideally). Next, *slowly* move your attention through your emotions, thoughts and physical sensations, scanning for how energized you feel and how tense you are in body and mind. Try not to hold expectations, and be willing to be surprised. Greet whatever you find with kindness and acceptance. Your fatigue, twitchy muscle, or irritation is neither bad nor good – it's simply your reality right now.

"When I started [yoga]," says Dominique Davis, "… the whole practice was 'How does that feel? Take a deep breath in. Notice the sensations. Notice the shift. Notice one side versus the other sides.' … The process of yoga was being aware. After a while it's just become intuitive."

In early scans, Dominique's ease will likely elude you. You may find that you're not sure what your body or feelings are telling you; or, you may minimize the intensity of what you do identify. Speedstress, like any habit, normalizes its own behaviors to some extent. Acupuncturist Ian Florian runs across this frequently in her clients. "They don't usually see that they're moving too fast. It's usually something that I would bring up," she says.

So, assume that what your scan reveals is impacting you more than it initially seems to be. After enough scans, you'll begin to notice gradations in your pace and your tension and energy levels. Other subtleties in your experience will also become apparent. When Melany Coopmans notices "a sense of urgency," she's learned to pay extra attention to what's happening in her heart and shoulders.

Because the body's sole time zone is the present, your scan will serve as the pathway returning you from *Next!* to *now*. The faster you move through your scan, the less you'll come into the present, so you may want to do as April Yvonne Garrett does. "I take some time listening to what my body's telling me, what my emotions are telling me," says April, the founder of a nonprofit and a website. "Generally that stuff is the core stuff and it really dissipates all the stuff that's not really *you*."

The l-step

The *l-step* invites you to listen to the "really *you*" identified in your scan. Only then can you effectively answer the question, *What's my slowlution?*

The correct answer in any particular moment is any activity (or lack of activity) that:

- is appropriate to your circumstances,
- helps you defocus from stressors, and/or
- moves you toward calm or a feeling of revitalization in mind, body or emotion.

No slowlution is too silly or quirky as long as, when focused on, it *works for you*. Christine O'Kelly finds that "appreciating the little things ... appreciating a picture that a 5-year-old draws,

The I-step

Using the information from your scan:

LISTEN for the answer to **What's my slowlution?**

Do you need to *calm down* or *rest*, or to *revitalize* your energy?

Early on, keep things simple: Select from a limited menu of slowlutions appropriate to your circumstances.

taking the time to say 'What is happening in this picture?'" proves a wonderful option for disengaging from speedstress.

Early on, I encourage you to keep things simple as you decide on your answer. Your tension and hurry may make it more difficult to know the way in which you want to slow down. As you can imagine, if you keep choosing and discarding the way in which you want to slow down, your tension will only mount. So, draw initially from a limited assortment of simple options that promise to calm you when you're tensely activated or to heighten your energy when you're tired.

Slowlutions for the first few weeks of practice

Moving from <u>tension</u> towards <u>calm</u>:

With focus …

- *Walk and/or breathe slowly,* focusing on the feel of your feet meeting the floor and on your incoming and outgoing breaths.

- *Visualize* being in a favorite or imagined soothing location (close your eyes, if it's safe or appropriate to do so).

- *Listen* with focus to soft, calming music (close your eyes, if possible).

- *Let go:* Sitting down, take a deep breath in as you gently raise your shoulders. As you exhale, drop your shoulders *slowly and gently*, letting that sense of release move down through your torso, drawing you into greater relaxation. Breathe gently and deeply.

- *Ground yourself:* Lie on the earth and feel its support; listen to birdsong; take in nature's beauty.

- *Exercise* so as to both distract yourself from stress and work off tension.

Moving from <u>tiredness</u> to a higher state of <u>energy</u>:

With focus …

- *Rest* or nap, if possible.

- *Move!* if that seems most revitalizing: Leap, dance, do jumping jacks …

- If your time is limited, *let go* (top of page); then, call in activating thoughts or memories.

- *Imagine* yourself an athlete jumping hurdles or running about on a tennis court (close your eyes, if appropriate).

- *Hum* or *sing* a rousing tune, letting its energy move through your body.

- *Eat* something healthy and energizing

Slowlutions for later weeks

As your familiarity with *i slow* increases, you'll still draw from calming or energizing ways to address speedstress' tension or tiredness.

"Warm baths, preferably with candles ..." and "transition time ... a few minutes between work and interacting with family" are a few of the calming slowlutions shared with me. Movement can be especially helpful in working off an excess of tension or re-sparking one's energy after sitting in one place as you work. "[If] you get up and move, it can be empowering in itself, like 'I can move, I can get up, I don't have to be stuck'," says psychologist Michelle Joshua, Ph.D. (Notice the increased sense of control suggested by "I don't have to be stuck," as well as the power of using the body to influence feelings.)

As slowing down feels more familiar, you may also want to consider whether your haste has left you feeling disconnected. Taking time with friends and partners is often a good distraction from stress. A one-to-one chat with a trusted friend can help settle one's anxieties, just as a laughter-filled outing can prove revitalizing.

With time, you'll find that the *I-step*'s question, *What's my slowlution?* will find its answer not only in you, but all around you. Opportunities for slowing down are everywhere. They hover around us like helpful ghosts, awaiting only our intention and focus to breathe life into them.

What's my slowlution?

≋ Practice the *s-step*. Taking a deep breath first is always a good idea.

≋ When you feel comfortable with the *s-step*, add the *l-step*. (You may well find that it follows seamlessly.) Let your scan guide your answer to *What's my slowlution?* External circumstances can guide you, as well; for example, what manner of slowing down does a long hallway or a red light suggest to you?

Chapter 13

Opt In: The *o-step*

"All I have to do to change the pace of my life is to choose to do so and then take action steps to do it."

~ Sarah

In the *o-step*, we exit speedstress' ever-turning wheel for a sweeter circle, the "o" of opting to enter into your chosen slowlution with focus.

Kathy Cooper opted to slow down after the death of two brothers in middle age made the necessity of a slower pace undeniable to her. "Neither of them knew that they were going to die...It was just 'here' and then 'gone'," Kathy says.

The o-step

OPT to enter into your slowlution for 30 seconds or more, with as much <u>focus</u> as is safely possible.

After those losses, Kathy, who designs and paints floor mats for a living, began attending more carefully to her choices. She took stock of her chronic illness, realizing "my body's more fragile than I think it is." This acknowledgement of what was real *for her* – a key slowing-down tool – led Kathy to the awareness that she needed to cut back on her pace of production. "My life," she told me, "is more important than something that somebody's going to put on the floor in their house."

Speedstress all too often leaves people feeling akin to one of Kathy's mats – flat, stepped-on, and helpless to change. Consequently, the *o-step*'s importance is two-fold. Each time you attentively follow through with a slow-down, you'll not only replace your haste and task-focus with a calming or energizing experience, you'll also know that you chose *for* your well-being.

Length of practice

Whatever your slowlution, decide on the length of time you intend for it, and follow through. While the latter may seem an obvious point, it's likely that your focus will waver and your anxiety about *not doing* will try to drag you out of your break and back to your to-dos. So, to ensure success during the first month of practice, don't ask too much of yourself: Set brief periods for your *o-step*. That might mean choosing thirty seconds, or three minutes, depending on your circumstances.

At shorter durations, a dramatic decrease in tension or up-surge in energy is not the most relevant, or realistic, outcome of your *o-step*. Yet, as we'll see, there will still be plenty of rewards to watch for.

There's no point in ever getting into a competition with yourself, or others, as to how long any slowlution lasts. Just as a seed's bounty far exceeds its physical dimensions, *i slow's* outcome over time will prove far richer than any measures of its duration. So, don't compare the length of one slow-down to another: Value 60 seconds of entering into one as much as you do 60 minutes. Each appreciation will not only lift your mood, it will infuse energy into your motivation to persist with habit change.

As you become more comfortable with slowing down, you will likely choose to lengthen your slowlutions; your shift toward calmer energy will become more evident then. With time and practice, as well, you'll eventually let go of *i slow* as your seed practice. You'll know when those moments have arrived. Keep in mind, however, that replacing a habitual behavior generally requires regular use of the new behavior over a period of time ranging from three weeks to approximately six months.

Focus!

"If your mind is tense," says meditation teacher Diana Salyer, "what you do is going to be that way."

The more you can invest your attention *in* your experience of slowing down, the less aware you'll be of stressors – and the calmer you'll feel. Robert Thayer, Ph.D. points to meditation as an example of this. "One of the reasons I think meditation works to reduce anxiety is it takes the focus of attention away from one's personal problems and [the] negative issues in one's life," he says.

During your slow-down, I encourage you to keep kindly returning your focus from its drift toward stressors so that you become as absorbed as is safely possible in either:

- your *in-the-body experience* of your slowlution (for example, when breathing deeply and slowly, focus on the sensation of your in- and out-breaths).
  or
- the *slowlution* itself (for example, engage as fully as is possible in a conversation or in watching the currents in a river).

As you become aware that your attention has drifted to what you're not getting done or to other thoughts about your life, you may experience a feeling of judgmental annoyance with yourself: *What's wrong with me? How hard can this be? I'm not doing this right.* Of course, that will not only increase your tense activation, it will make you far less likely to persist in slowing down. So, rather than feeding that reaction by lingering with it, kindly note its presence and choose to move on. Remind yourself that even the minds of the most experienced meditators can wander – that's a fact. Kindly cultivate a sense of normalcy around losing one's focus as you first slow down. *Of course this isn't easy – I'm breaking a habit of focusing on stressors. In fact, it's great that I noticed my focus veering off from my slowlution because that allows me to re-gather it.*

Then, do just that. Imagine your arms lightly and kindly gathering your attention back to the *here* and *now*. Drift, gather … drift, gather. "Recognize that you just went somewhere," says Jane Lubischer after years of practicing Tai Chi. "Say 'O.K., I was thinking. Come back.' No judgment, no blame, no disappointment, no shame. Just bring it back. And the more you do that, the better you get at staying in the moment."

If a nagging noise or visual stimuli keeps drawing your attention away, incorporate it into your practice. For example, when a droning piece of machinery is unavoidably close, you might choose to let your slowlution morph to the memory of a beach, where the droning can help recreate the sound of the surf. Turn distractions into assets as much as you possibly can. And, even when only a minimal focus is possible because of your circumstances, give yourself credit for doing what you can to ease your speedstress.

Each time you kindly refocus on slowing down, you'll weaken stress' habitual hold on your attention because you're using your brain differently. As it becomes easier over time to sustain your focus, you will increasingly realize that, despite your speedstressed self-talk, you really are fine in the present moment: You are not in an emergency and your worry is speculation, rather than a present reality. You are simply here, with yourself, fully inhabiting the present, the only moment of time you ever have.

"If you can control your mind that way, you can apply it in any different situation," notes Jane. When you turn your attention back to your to-do's, you'll prove a better resource, with your focus more attuned to what's in front of you *now*, rather than on what's still to be done.

What's my slowlution?

➲ Put the *s-*, *l-* and *o-steps* into practice, briefly at first.

➲ Imagine yourself in an especially speedstressed and/or public circumstance. Then, figure out a slowlution you could use that's appropriate for even that extreme situation.

Chapter 14

Watch Actively for Rewards:
The w-step

"I had little twinges of an old feeling that life could be an adventure, that it __was__ an adventure."

~ Jolene Robinson, R.N.

Sitting next to a river after a deadening day at work, Jolene Robinson let her attention relax into the water's movement and sound, into the shelter of the trees bordering the river. Afterwards, she

The w-step

WATCH actively
for rewards from
slowing down.

watched for the rewards (*w-step*). In addition to reconnecting with life's potential for adventure, she recalls, "I felt a little lighter and a little more creative."

If you actively watch for rewards, reader, you will find them.

Even Sarah, who opted for a slow-down that many might view as speedstress-inducing, actively noticed rewards. "One day, I took time to JUST drive to do my errands (I didn't talk on the phone or eat or make notes at red lights. I just drove)," Sarah writes. "This was very relaxing and impacted my whole day positively."

Sarah not only identified that she felt more relaxed, she kept watching for rewards; as a result, her slowlution's effect lingered, weaving an altered experience of her day.

As a beginner, though, be realistic. While your speedstressed self will want to feel calmer or more energized *right now*, those rewards will likely arrive on a more recalcitrant timetable. After early *o-steps*, you may not notice much movement toward calmer energy.

Even so, there are always rewards to be had from *i slow*, or any form of slowing down. So, as you begin practicing, *actively* watch for one or more. Such witnessing is crucial to letting go of any habit because, as you'll recall, rewards encourage us to continue building new behaviors.

Early rewards

What, then, are the goodies that even your first practice of *i slow* will yield?

Self-respect: It's interesting to note that the Latin root for the word "respect" means "to look back at" or "regard." The *s-step's* scan and the act of listening in the *l-step* offer you the chance to, quite literally, hold yourself in a new regard after being focused on tasks. Because speedstress typically causes people to feel that they are lacking in relation to both their tasks and their relationships, an increase in one's self-respect is an important and healing reward.

Not rushing: Remind yourself that during the seconds or minutes you were slowing down, you were not moving in haste. In other words, you weren't *reinforcing* your speedstress habit; nor were you allowing your lists, boss, or worries to run you.

Increased sense of control: Acting on your intention will provide a much needed boost to your sense of personal control. "When people feel more control they respond better to stress," says researcher Shevaun D. Neupert, Ph.D. "It's a very beneficial buffer. Feeling like you're an active agent and the things that you do matter to help bring about goals and desired outcomes is very, very important."

While in the midst of caring for her twins, Rebecca learned to prompt herself to "take a minute, take a breath and figure out what you need or what you want." As a result, she began to feel increasingly masterful and in control. "It's given me a chance to pay attention more … I've honed in more on the kind of person that I feel like is inside, and how I make that person be."

Absence of feared consequences: In the *w-step*, be sure to check in as to whether any of the consequences you feared from slowing down actually materialized? In the unlikely event that they did, how significant were they? Most likely, your answers will belie your fears. Take good note: This is evidence you can call up when anxious thinking threatens to keep you spinning on speedstress' wheel.

Cheerlead: Create your own reward by rooting for yourself immediately after completing the *o-step*. *Way to go!*, you might want to say; or, perhaps, a quieter affirmation will appeal: *I just did something good for myself. I'm glad about that.* Doing so may at first seem awkward, but what you are actually accomplishing – positive reinforcement – is entirely necessary for habit-change.

Signs of change: If you prefer visible reminders of your accomplishment, hang a sheet of paper on the wall, or keep a document on your desktop. Draw a seed (or insert a seed-symbol) each time you practice *i slow*. Seed by seed, you'll draw your new pace into being.

Later rewards

With practice established for several weeks or months, you should begin to note increased ease and well-being. Perhaps you notice that your pace has slowed, helping you to remain calmer; your energy may be better. You may be working smarter, rather than faster. Check in as to whether there's been a shift in how you relate to others. Are you listening more closely, or laughing more? Perhaps you're experiencing your child's goodnight hug in a new way.

You may increasingly recognize the large gifts present in small moments. The beauty of nature will likely crystallize from its previous blur. Perhaps you are more able to lose yourself in a relaxing visualization or you've started pausing before responding to requests. How are you sleeping, eating, feeling? Watch for changes in your speedstressed self-talk and in your ability to be kind to yourself and patient with others.

Surprise rewards

Be sure to watch for rewards that manifest in ways you would never have predicted. As Marcy Litle's process of slowing down unfolded over the years, it sparked a redefinition of what success meant to her. "I refused the notion that work was my whole life, that I owed it all of my time," she says. "…Success is having your own life and being present to it."

Other unexpected benefits may range from weight loss (eating more slowly, you'll become aware of fullness earlier on in the meal) to finding a new home (after noticing a for-sale sign you might previously have hurried by). Take note when a friend offers you feedback that, for example, you seem more rested or less hurried.

Rewards shine from almost anywhere as long as we slow down to look for them. Zelda Lockhart experienced just this one sunny morning. A flat tire interrupted Zelda's progress through errands, causing her to pull over to the side of road to wait for a tow truck. Her enforced slow time was not at first welcome, but its rewards soon became evident. "At first I was totally freaked out," recalls Zelda. "And then I realized how beautiful of a day it was, and it wasn't so bad sitting there waiting on the tow truck. And I realized I drive by this place every day and I never knew that there was wild carrot growing there."

The gift Zelda received that day carried on. She began watching for wild carrots and she found them, pushing, like green promises, through cracked asphalt as she walked her daughter to school.

What's my slowlution?

‿ If you haven't already, begin practicing the five steps of *i slow* - four times a day.

‿ Make a cheat-sheet of the rewards to be had in early practice; then, actively watch for them – and others.

Cultivating Calm

Relating Anew to Anxiety

Chapter 15

Yikes! The Power of Thought

"The mind can really dictate your life out of control ... It's what's up here in your head that's creating this world that you're living in."

~ Dominique Davis

Looking back, Christine O'Kelly can see the power her thinking had over her pace. "The way I was thinking about my life was dictating what I was going to do with my body," Christine O'Kelly recalls. "I would not slow down at work. I would stay up too late. I would take in way too much caffeine. It was a terrible cycle."

We have long known that culture shapes language; emerging research demonstrates that words themselves affect how we see the world. Psychologist Lera Boroditsky of Stanford University has conducted studies that show that words' genders in languages such as French or German, or the description of a single object by multiple words in one language, can affect the native speaker's perceptions and thoughts.

While it's tempting to write off our inner chatter, or self-talk, as meaningless, it is far from that. Harnessing your mind will play an important role in slowing down. As you learn to recognize and rework thoughts that boost your anxiety, shifting your habitual patterns will become easier. If, on the other hand, your self-talk frames your circumstances as depriving you of any choice about your pace, you will feel less empowered to make the changes you want.

You can hear this understandable, but unhelpful, mental stance in a comment from a male survey-respondent, "Sean." "The endless tasks never go away. Just more gets added," Sean writes. "My business requires a lot of attention even from home. At home, things always need maintenance or fixing ... The constant input of new information of every sort overwhelms and paralyzes as it is impossible to pay attention or do it all ... Yikes!"

Sean's "Yikes!" both underlines and reinforces his sense of helplessness. In fact, according to the research of psychiatrist David Burns, MD, a thought can elicit a feeling in less than one second. Unfortunately for Sean, "Yikes!" does nothing to encourage feelings of self-confidence or empowerment. Those feelings are inspired, however, by another male survey-taker as he describes what's most helpful in learning to slow down: "I can stop and think about what's really important."

Not only is this a true statement, it affirms personal mastery (resources) in the midst of demands. When you consider the power of thought in light of the fact that our experience of stress rises and falls to a large degree on our perceptions, it becomes clear that working with self-talk is crucial to healing speedstress.

Recognizing accelerating self-talk

But, how do you even recognize the familiar – even, automatic - commentaries that glint through your mind like quicksilver, accelerating your pace and tense activation? As we'll see, identifying the presence of such *accelerators* is the first step toward determining their type. Once you know the latter, you can choose a "decelerating" thought-strategy that helps you slow down and move toward calmer energy.

The following clues can suggest that an accelerating thought has just flashed through your mind:

Feelings

As soon as you notice that you are feeling stressed, anxious, fearful, helpless or overwhelmed in relation to your tasks or to slowing down, turn your distress into a tool for discovery: Ask yourself, *What did I just tell myself? What was I just thinking?* While situational issues may play a role in how you're feeling, you also likely had a thought about those.

Your pace

Similarly, when you become aware that you are walking or moving quickly, pose the question, *Why am I rushing? What am I telling myself about* [being late … my demands, etc.]? You may get some surprising answers. After Rhonda Miller spent some time exploring how her busy-ness and hasty pace intersected with her personal history, she became clear that, underlying all the obvious influences, "I'm trying to rush everything to see how much I can get in today or tomorrow to cheat death in some way."

Bodily experience

Let your body be your guide, as well. If you realize, for example, that you're starving or urgently need to visit the bathroom, inquire – kindly! - as to what mindset might have caused you to miss or override signs of physical need. Imbalanced self-care can mean that your inner commentary is not supporting it.

The words you speak

The words we speak often offer unintended clues to our inner perspective. So, listen to what you say to others about your pace and your ability to change it. For instance, are you prone to proclaiming, like the bookstore customer we met earlier, that hurrying is "the story of our lives"?

Whenever you hear yourself spouting an accelerating phrase, be glad. In that moment, your mind has stepped outside of its habitual patterns enough to recognize such self-talk.

Reality, not rules

As you become more aware of your accelerators, you'll realize that some of them are so entrenched and long-standing that they function like rules. As a first step to loosening the grip of these "rules," replace them with realistic statements that instill calmer energy. The new statements will initially feel less true to you than the rules, but just keep using them. See if you have any "rules" or "realities" to add to the list on the next page.

After your initial reading of the list, read each column separately. Do you notice a difference in tone between the two? The rules tend toward extreme pronouncements, narrowing one's options, while the realities tend to be calming and encouraging of balance.

It's probably also clear that some of the rules are quite judgmental. When steeped in demands that never seem to end, it is easy to believe that we're somehow lacking. Unfortunately, self-judgment causes tension and negative emotional activation. Consequently, it is the first accelerating line of self-talk that we'll look at revising.

Accelerating Rule	Reality
I have to do everything.	I'll do what I calmly can right now.
I can't stop to [eat, sleep, etc.]	My body has limits.
Tasks trump my needs.	Even machinery gets regular maintenance.
I'm worthless if I'm not busy.	Slowing down will help me know mysef differently.
Slowing down is impossible.	I have control over my pace and my focus.
If it's on the list, it needs doing now.	I can prioritize.
Having needs is weak	I'm designed for balance.
I have no choice but to…	Even prisoners have choice.
I'm always behind – I'm useless!	I'm expecting too much of myself.
When I retire, I'll enjoy myself.	Time is not a given.
I have to rush to make up time.	Time is not expandable; options are.
I can relax after.	There will always be more to do.
I'll never find work if I rest	Rested, I'll offer the best impression.

Accelerator: Judgment

Rebecca Barbee noticed judgments sliding her way after she quit work to raise her infant twins. "We're not that busy and I feel like that really throws people off when you say you're not," Rebecca says. "They're like 'Something's wrong with you. You're not busy. You should be busy'."

Some people stay on the run to stay ahead of others' - or their own - critical evaluations. This self-talk is extremely unkind, eating away at self-esteem and ratcheting up tension. Our ability to view our self as a positive resource in the context of our dilemma declines.

If you entertain judgmental thoughts (as many people do), changing your pace may well ignite a ratcheting-up of self-criticism. "I have an internalized voice, 'You're being lazy, you're not driven enough, you're stupid'," says Kerry Johnson of her experience when she first slowed down.

Beware the duplicity of such thinking! Negative judgments are nothing more than emotion-driven opinions that are expressed in a way that makes them sound factual. They aren't. Rather than being calm, measured evaluations of fact that encourage us to explore positive change, judgments are descriptors that shape-shift according to our mood and circumstances. They pack a demoralizing emotional wallop.

Judgments can become so automatic that we don't notice them. As soon as you do become aware that you're criticizing yourself or others, refrain from judging yourself for it! Instead, be grateful that you noticed. Only then can you begin to revise this unhelpful thinking.

Decelerators: Self-judgment

Characteristics: Non-judgment separates fact from opinion; invites learning and positive change, rather than a loss of self-esteem. An absence of judgment reduces negative activation, making calmness and kindness more possible.

Putting the brakes on self-judgment

Peel, reveal, and deal: Peel (judgmental opinion) to _reveal_ (the facts) in order to _deal_ effectively (with the facts). This process will take you from feeling swamped in negative opinion to an empowering consideration of what's real.

To illustrate, we'll use _peel_, _reveal_, and _deal_ (_P, R & D_) on judgments two interviewees shared with me.

- *P, R & D #1*: Kerry's self-judgment, "You're being lazy, you're not driven enough, you're stupid."

Kerry's words offer powerful illustration of how negative opinion leads us away from a state of calm. Would Kerry's self-judgment encourage her to problem-solve? No. When we don't feel good about ourselves, we are less likely to feel confident and motivated. As so often happens with negative judgment, Kerry had made *herself* the problem. Defining ourselves as flawed sends an implicit message of *I have little ability to improve this situation.*

Now, let's *peel* (the judgmental opinion), *reveal* (the facts) so that we can *deal* effectively (with those facts).

Peel: Identify the opinion; then, peel it from the statement.

If sorting opinions out feels challenging, pay special attention to words that "describe," rather than state, facts. Adjectives and adverbs describe, as do any extreme characterizations (calling oneself "a sloth," for example). In Kerry's comment, the opinions/descriptors are "lazy," "driven enough," and "stupid." To *peel*, drop those words. What are you left with?

"You're being – you're not – you're… ".

What once seemed a powerful statement of fact has been reduced to a series of gaping holes! Yet, what's to say the opinion wasn't based on facts? To answer that, let's reveal them.

Reveal: Ask yourself, *What are the facts?*

Here, you uncover the actual facts or circumstances as they relate to each part of the judgment. The purpose of *reveal* is to either put the lie to your judgment or to make your judgment-inducing misstep more understandable. As it happens, Kerry shared some facts with me that contradict each negative descriptor:

- "Lazy" - *The facts*: Kerry had been working long hours for years. So much for lazy!
- "Driven enough" - *The facts:* Kerry told me that her change in pace was driven by a real desire: "Instead of working to earn a living I want to live." It's a fact that Kerry isn't as driven to work as she used to be, but that doesn't mean she isn't "driven enough"; her motivation has simply changed. (What is driven *enough*, anyway? Beware *enough* – it's often *should* disguised as an adverb.)
- "Stupid" - *The facts*: Kerry has a Master's Degree; she helps others sort out their lives. That surely puts the lie to this opinion.

Deal: Ask yourself, *Given these facts, how can I deal most effectively with* [the circumstance that sparked the initial judgment, which, here = *slowing down*]?

Kerry might now tell herself, 'It's a fact that I'm not driven in my work life right now. I want to slow down in order to put my energy into really living. That fact has nothing to do with my intelligence, which earned me a Master's.' This calm, measured evaluation would be far more helpful to Kerry than her original statement.

Peel, Reveal, and Deal

Peel the opinionated/ descriptive words from the judgmental statement.

Reveal the formerly obscured facts by asking, *What are the facts?*

Deal in a balanced manner with your present circumstance: *Given these facts, how can I deal most effectively with ...?*

As *peel*, *reveal*, and deal makes clear, negative opinions leave us feeling one-down, rather than effective. Facts, on the other hand, provide us realistic choices.

- *P R, & D #2*: I met with Dan after he had been laid off for a year. He was feeling discouraged about his job hunt. His judgment: "I tell myself 'OK, well, I was good at my job but I'm really not good for much of anything else'."

You can imagine how anxiety-provoking such self-talk is when someone is looking for work. So, let's *peel, reveal* and *deal*:

Peel: Identify the opinion; then, peel it from the judgmental statement. "...really not good for much of anything else" would be peeled. No facts are lurking in that undergrowth of description, are they? This leaves "I tell myself 'Ok, well, I was good at my job, but I'm ..." True, the "good" in the remaining statement appears to be an opinion, but I'm leaving it in because it's a proven fact. Dan's employer, a major corporation, spent money to transfer him across country; he worked with them for decades, transforming "a research project into a successful business."

Dan's *P, R & D* could stop right with "O.K., well, I was good at my job." When the judgmental statement came up in his mind again (as they do), he could remind himself as to why he was successful. But, we'll continue so as to illustrate *reveal* and *deal* again.

Reveal: *What are the facts?* Look for the facts formerly obscured by the opinion.

"Not good for much of anything else" - The facts: Dan had the smarts to get a Ph.D., which means he has the smarts to adjust to new, and possibly different, work. In fact, since being laid off, Dan has already done this. He took and passed a course to become a real estate agent. The harsh judgment is not only harmful to Dan's confidence, it's also untrue.

Deal: *Given these facts, how can I deal most effectively with* [the job hunt]?

Having revealed his own success and capability in the step above, Dan might become increasingly aware of what's at the core of his anxiety about finding employment. As we talked, Dan shared that "I don't really know what I want to do." This reality – an entirely normal one after a lay-off - provides a starting point for discovery.

Evaluating, rather than judging, Dan might now say, 'No judgment can erase the talents and abilities that made me good at my last job. I already know I can learn new skills. I have to make a decision about what I want to do. How can I deal with that as effectively as possible?'

Can you find anything that is not fact-based in that statement?

Now, imagine you are waking up in the morning with a day of job-searching ahead of you. Run Dan's judgment through your mind, and then the factual statement. Which would most help you present yourself calmly and effectively?

Two other strategies for working with self-judgment may also prove effective:

Reverse the Golden Rule: We are often far kinder to those we love than we are to our self. So, flip the Golden Rule: Tell yourself, *Do unto myself as I would have myself do unto others.* Just as you would when others make a mistake or let themselves down, respond kindly, positively, and realistically. Remind yourself that you, like everyone, are imperfect in your actions, but worthy in your essence.

The Learning Tool: No situation or action that incites self-judgment is ever a loss if we can learn from it; in fact, wisdom is in large part derived from what we make of our stumbles. When you rebuke yourself, make a shift: Ask yourself, *What can I learn from this?* Let the learning move you from tense negativity to positive growth.

As you interact more kindly with yourself, you'll not only do so with others, you'll be more inclined to ease up on your stress-inducing pace. (Take note, though: As with slowing down, revising judgmental self-talk takes time and practice.)

As you read through the accelerators and decelerators in the upcoming chapter, take note of those that seem most relevant for you.

What's my slowlution?

- Begin tracing back from clues provided by your pace, body, feelings or statements in order to identify any speedstress-inducing self-talk.

- Begin to listen for self-judgment. Apply one of the decelerators. Remember that judgment, like speedstress, can become habitual. Keep working with it.

Chapter 16

Putting the Brakes On:
Revising Self-Talk

*"Haste can lead to failure. Not giving yourself time to think
things through can lead to mistakes that you regret later."*

~ Iziah Barden

As a young mother, Rhonda Miller found herself in a "horrendous" situation: She was working full-time and, at night, she
was breastfeeding her baby. As a result, she became extremely
sleep-deprived. She continued in this pattern, she told me,
"because it seemed like that's the way things were supposed to be
done if someone wanted to keep up with their career."

Rhonda's thinking about how she was "supposed to" live was
accelerating her pace. Below, we'll take a look at coercive self-talk
and other accelerators.

Accelerator: <u>Coercion</u>

Coercive language (*supposed to, should, ought to, need to, have
to, have no choice*, etc.) robs us of a sense of choice and empowerment. As in Rhonda's case, it can over-focus us on what we
believe needs to be done, to the exclusion of what we want or
what's true for us physically or emotionally.

Coercive themes can also be speedstress-inducing for those not in the workforce. A year into her retirement, Shelley Beason still has moments of telling herself, "I need to be productive, I need to have something to show at the end of my day." (Take heart, reader: Shelley can now laugh at this line of thought.)

With this accelerator we tell our self that we must bridge the unbridgeable: We should be able to stretch *too little* to handle *too much*, rather than brainstorming how to reprioritize, ask for help, or recharge ourselves.

Decelerators: Coercion

Characteristics: Decelerating self-talk enhances your sense of choice, control or empowerment in relation to time, tasks, or resources; it widens your recognition of options and resources beyond those suggested by a "should" or "have to."

Putting the brakes on

Says who? Pose this question to coercive self-talk. The answer will often be, *Well ... er ... only me!* Reframe your relationship to the dilemma in a way that puts you more in charge.

- Ex: *No one but me is saying I have to hurry. I can choose to move more slowly.*

What are my options? When considering your dilemma, ask yourself this question. It will widen your perspective and help you identify more choices than your coercive self-talk implied.

Should to good: At times, an obligation *does* have to be done *right now*. *True* last-minute work deadlines, pick-ups from day-care, physical emergencies, and securing income when your bank account is near rock-bottom belong in this category. However, you can still take charge of *how* you approach your responsibility.

Mentally resisting the task at hand will only increase any stress you're experiencing. Instead, offer yourself some control by asking, How can I turn *'should' to 'good'?* If there's even the slightest window of time, reach for the *good*: Prime yourself to approach your required task as calmly and effectively as possible.

- Ex: You might choose to take a few deep breaths, eat a quick snack, make a list of your options, or re-frame your "have to" as a benefit to you.

Accelerator: <u>Extreme Language</u>

Extreme descriptors powerfully impact us. Words such as *never, always, hopeless,* and common sayings such as *This is a disaster* or *I'll die if...*, tend to either inflate the negative or deflate the resources at hand. Coercive verbs often characterize situations in extreme turns.

When the mind goes to extremes, it often jacks up negative emotional activation and, so, our experience of stress. As a result, we become tense, but feel disempowered to do much about the stressor.

Executive Mary Bennett's belief that "good work now means...you're on top of everything" offers an example of this accelerator. We can surely stay on top of a few things, but every-thing? Such language obscures the fact that life's circumstances usually inhabit the realm between extremes.

Take these descriptors, which often include self-judgments, as clues that you are likely interpreting your dilemma in unreal-istic terms. After all, even the most unnerving of circumstances, such as losing one's job, are not emergencies each and every moment. In fact, many challenges that truly are extreme can't be solved in a day. It's stress-inducing to rush about as if they could be.

Decelerators: Extreme Language

Characteristics: These decelerators avoid extreme characterizations; reduce negative emotional activation; acknowledge that, while success may occasionally benefit from brief excursions into extremes of effort, balance is necessary to sustain overall well-being.

Putting the brakes on

Where's the middle? … Where's balance? Pose these questions. Like plants that thrive under normal rainfall rather than droughts or flooding, we sustain ourselves from moderate thinking. You'll shift to center as you remind yourself that your circumstance will pass, or that options or resources you hadn't considered exist.

'Seeming' rather than 'extreming': Add "*seems*" in front of extreme language as you talk to yourself. "Seems overwhelming" has a different feel than "is overwhelming," doesn't it? "Seems" invites a "but" that can serve as a doorway to positive alternatives or empowering language.

Accelerator: _Dire Outcomes_

Often, anxiety-laden thinking links reasonable self-care to catastrophic outcomes. *If I slow down, I'll lose my friends' respect … If I slow down, I'll never find a job.* (Notice the use of the extreme "never;" we often incorporate several accelerators into one line of self-talk.)

Consider reality, however: Because most of life plays out in the middle, any extreme outcome from sensibly slowing down is, by definition, not very likely to occur.

Filtered through more balanced thought, the notion that sensible slowlutions can threaten job security or identity seems far less compelling. Slowing down and success - as a person or an employee - don't have to be mutually exclusive.

<u>Decelerators</u>: Dire Outcomes

Characteristics: Considers anxiety about changing your pace in the context of the talents, attributes, and common sense you will bring to that process.

Putting the brakes on

How likely: Ask yourself, *As long as I'm slowing down sensibly, how likely is* [dire outcome]? Unless speed is part of your job description as, say, an ambulance driver, the negative outcome is probably not likely.

Let me count the reasons: Title a blank piece of paper with the completed phrase: *My biggest fear is that* [dire outcome] *will happen when I slow down.* Draw a line down the middle of the sheet. On the left side, write all the ways in which you believe your speedstress is helpful in preventing the feared outcome. Next, think through all your non-speedstressed abilities and attributes, and all the actions you could take, that would serve to either prevent that outcome or lessen its effect.

- Ex: *When I slow down, my biggest fear is that I'll feel a lot of loneliness.*

How speedstress prevents loneliness	How I could prevent/lessen loneliness
Hurry makes me not notice how I'm feeling.	I could reach out to friends during some *i slow* breaks.
I'm so tired out, it makes me not care about being alone ... ETC.	I could use skills from the upcoming Anxiety chapter ... ETC.

Compare the lists. Does the right-hand column offer you some perspective, as well as some ideas? If the left hand list is longer, what does that say to you?

Accelerator: <u>Denial or Devaluation of Personal Reality</u>

Denial, or devaluation, of feelings, needs, and lifelong yearnings often lies at the heart of a speedstressed life. Thoughts about obligations and chores often contribute to this accelerator, obscuring awareness of our wants in the moment.

<u>Decelerators:</u> *Denial/Devaluation*

Characteristics: These decelerators acknowledge that two differing realities (for ex., demands *and* your personal needs) can exist at the same time. They encourage recognition of the interconnectedness of balanced self-care and sustainable goal-fulfillment.

Putting the brakes on

The AND rule: As soon as you recognize an accelerating thought, restate it and add on one of the two broadening phrases below:

1. "... *AND right now **I*** [*current physical/mental/or emotional experience*]."

- Ex: *I have way too much to do AND right now **I** am very tired.*

Next, sit with the extended sentence. What slowlution does it suggest?

OR, after restating an accelerator, add:

2. "*AND right now **I can decide to*** [*slowlution*]."

- Ex: *I'm totally overwhelmed AND right now I can decide to prioritize some of this.*

Next, enact your choice.

It's just a fact: As you realize that, despite all you have to do, your mind, body or feelings are speaking up, say to yourself: *It's just a fact that I* [*personal reality*].

- Ex: *It's just a fact that I'm missing my child ... hungry ... in need of exercise ...*

The phrase invites you to open your mind to working out a way to attend to both your demands and your personal reality.

Accelerator: Worry thoughts

Worry accelerates our tension and it tires us out; it is rarely effective. In fact, as Stelle Shumann looks back at the time when she was routinely speedstressed, she realizes that "it wasn't the work that made me stressed. It was the internal worrying."

Nonetheless, greet this type of thinking with great kindness – your psyche means well. In the face of an unknown – for example, *How am I going to get all this done?* or *When will I find work?* – worrying is an attempt to figure out a solution and maintain a sense of control. That may explain why it is easy for us to fall into believing that worry is useful. Usually, quite the opposite is true: When we make a habit of priming ourselves for negative outcomes or trying to foresee the unforeseeable future, we only end up trapping ourselves in tension.

Decelerators: Worry thoughts

When you notice that anxious rumination about all you have to do is making you tense and tired, put some of the following strategies to use (if worrying has become habitual, as it frequently does, seek professional help):

- *Challenge the logic* underlying your worry thoughts: Given what you know about the situation and about life in general, how likely is it *really* that the feared outcome will occur? Be sure and ask a calm confidant for their perspective.

- If your worry does have some logic to it, ask yourself, *Have I done everything I can to prevent, or to reduce the likelihood of, X happening?* If you haven't, do it now as best you can. Then, greet subsequent worry thoughts with *I've done everything that I can.*

- Remind yourself that worry deals with what isn't real – and may never be. Tell yourself, *The future isn't real. If I calm myself by focusing on here and now, I'll have more mental energy on hand should the problem actually occur.*

Once you've determined that the worry is either illogical or that you've done everything you can, distract youself:

- *Stop sign*: When you recognize a worry, picture a red stop sign popping up to halt the thought's progress, or say "stop." Then, distract with an engrossing activity.

- *Leaf*: Scoop your worry thoughts up, one by one, and place each on a leaf floating down a stream. Let them move out of your consciousness in this peaceful manner. Repeat as needed.

Accelerator: <u>Helpless and/or Alone</u>

People newly shorn of their jobs often feel keenly the loss of social interaction the workplace afforded. "Pretty soon you don't talk to the people you work[ed] with … They're still working so hard," says Carol Shaw. Self-talk that emphasizes one's aloneness often increases stress and lowers mood, as well as making the retired vulnerable to overbooking themselves.

On the other extreme, the belief that one has so much to do at work that interaction with one's colleagues isn't possible can also create stress. When I asked Dave Banner, the San Francisco purchasing executive, what one thing he'd like to get out of this book, he replied, "that I'm not alone in feeling like the stress is too much. People don't talk about it, they just *do*."

Self-talk that paints a picture of oneself as alone often invites self-judgment: *What's wrong with me? I just can't hack it. Everyone else seems energized and O.K.* Isolation and judgment, in turn, act to increase a sense of helplessness, making reaching out feel riskier.

Decelerators: _Helpless and/or Alone_

Characteristics: Reduces isolation and self-judgment; encourages networking and time with loved ones.

Chances are: Tell yourself, _Chances are, I'm not the only one feeling this way._ Or, _Chances are, I can find others in my situation._ This line of self-talk will make it easier to reach out to others. When you do, form a slowing circle (see Chapter 11). Support each other in noticing – and using – opportunities to slow down.

Take lunch: Create a standing lunch-date with someone who is also in transition. Swap tips, celebrate successes, and share the tough times. Brainstorm ways to slow down from stress or to decelerate your thinking.

Before Stelle learned to slow down, she, like many speedstressed people, paid a heavy price for her unwitting entrapment in accelerating thoughts and beliefs. At times, she told herself that her work took priority over attending personal events important to her husband. Then, he died. "I remember when he was dying, thinking about all that I missed out on, and it was too late. It was too late," she says.

Now living by a different set of beliefs, Stelle meditates and works from a home office. She's learned a powerful – and decelerating – truth: Taking brief intervals to slow down "can be done by simply doing it, making an effort to do it."

What's my slowlution?

‿ Identify at least one category of accelerating self-talk that contributes to your anxious rush. Write it down. Apply some tools from this chapter. Be sure to compare the inner effects of the accelerating and decelerating lines of self-talk.

‿ Quickly finish this sentence: *If I slow down from speed-stress_____.* Is a Dire Consequence present? Begin to pay attention to all the ways this belief shows up in your self-talk.

Chapter 17

On Positivity and Time: Growing New Thinking

"You're going to push to get everything done, but at what cost?
That's always an interesting question:
Are you going to get everything done off the list at the expense
of your own sanity, or somebody else's … ?"

~ Claudia Horwitz

Positivity: Moving from Ugh to Aaaah

A positive mood is a resource in and of itself. "When you experience a negative emotion, your focus narrows," says psychologist Michelle Joshua. "This is why when we're angry … we can't find a lot of solutions for a problem, but when we can relax our mood or start to feel better our perspective widens."

There's a simple but powerful reason for this: Just as thoughts influence our feelings, our moods affect what happens in our brain. Positive psychology, a relatively new lens through which to view human behavior, uses everything from film clips to meditative energy in order to elicit differing emotions and their effects. Positive emotions have been shown to prompt the recognition of broader visual patterns (seeing a triangle, say, rather than the component shapes forming it). In the throes of a good mood, we are able to more easily move from what is to what could be, making creative connections that enhance problem-solving and innovation.

Ironically, stress has resulted in Keith Spring understanding the power of positivity. "If there's something that you do have to do, you can do it 'Ugh' or you can do it 'Aaaah'," says Keith. "You really do have that choice, as tough as it might seem … We may be prisoners of situations but our response is not mandated, we can respond in a variety of ways."

Reaching for real positives – not Pollyanna-ish ones – doesn't require the denial of any real negatives. It simply allows the two to co-exist, fostering greater balance in one's outlook and making one less vulnerable to feeling overwhelmed. A positive approach – *O.K., there's got to be a way to get this done without rushing* – will help you not only reach for slowlutions, but also feel more in control.

But here's the catch: Our brains are primed to give more attention to the negative than the positive (probably to help us recognize threats to survival). Because of this, Barbara Frederickson, a pre-eminent positivity researcher, has reached the conclusion that we thrive

From Ugh to Aaaah

When you feel discouraged about slowing down:

Briefly acknowledge your discouragement – it's real, after all.

Example: *I've been racing around all week. It's not easy to remember to slow down.*

Make room for the positive:

- *Imagine your mind expanding out from the negative thought* (picture your mind as an inflatable balloon or imagine it's borders stretching o-u-t like a rubber band).

- Then, *open your mind* to what's real and encouraging:

Examples:

What helped me slow down when I was doing it consistently?

I practiced i slow for 2 weeks in a row before, so I have proof that I can do it again.

Persistence – not perfection - is the key to habit change.

when we experience positive emotions three times more than we do negative ones.

Three times more?, you may exclaim, *I have a hard enough time feeling <u>one</u> good feeling when I'm speedstressed!* Here, we return to the notion of balance. Because most of life is a complex mix of circumstances, positives usually exist in tandem with the negatives. We can train ourselves to make them out. In fact, watching for rewards in the *w-step* is designed to help you do just that.

Cultivating Positivity

Choose your focus

Where we choose to put our attention powerfully affects our emotions and thoughts and, so, our experience in any moment.

With clients, I often use the example of a carpet that has a stain on it. If you choose to focus on the blemish, it will become your experience of the rug, and unpleasant feelings and thoughts are sure to arise. If, however, you consider the carpet as a whole, you will also be able to appreciate its color and design. And, as we've just discussed, once you feel better, your mind will open: Perhaps there's a way to cover the stain or, even, get it out?

To search for positivity in the context of slowing down, you might, for example, wrap up chores or work by only *briefly* acknowledging that there's more to be done. That's true, but it's also true that there is work you *did* get done. Appreciatively take note of that reality. When feeling overwhelmed by your dilemma, move your focus from its demands to the resources you can call on. Such shifts from *Ugh* to *Aaaah* will move you toward calm, rather than toward stress.

Call on your mirror neurons

We can slow down and create positive experiences, improving our – and others' – moods. To do this, call on the talents of your mirror neurons:

Offer others the calm that they – and you! – want to feel. Our bodies and mental states are intricately connected. Use that reality to your advantage. "If you act hurried you'll feel hurried, and if you feel hurried you'll act hurried," says Steve Muth. "So even if you are hurried, don't act it, walk don't run and if you do run, run for fun." Speak calmly; smile, and walk at an easy pace – even if it feels like an act. Your mirror neurons will flash "ease" and other people's will signal back.

Seek out someone who behaves as you wish to feel: If even acting positive or calm seems beyond you, seek out someone who is often that way. Let yourself simply be in their presence. Breathe calmly; take in and appreciate their way of being (refrain from comparing their ease to how you've been feeling). Notice how you feel when you leave.

Offer attentiveness and interest: We all want to be heard and seen. Luckily, this works in everyone's favor when you slow down. As a grounding slowlution, offer your full presence during interactions. Gently guide your thoughts away from tasks; listen carefully, take in others' body language, expressions, and tone of voice – all sources of vital information. Respond thoughtfully. The people with whom you interact may not consciously know that your focused attention is soothing to them, but they will know that they like being around you.

Re-thinking Time

"I like the things I do, I just need more time," writes Sarah. "I know I cannot make my days longer or add more days to my weekend."

Sarah's realistic take is unusual. Most speedstressed thinking veers wide of reality on the topic of time - and understandably so: Time is amorphous. For all the specificity of our measurement of a day's 24 hours, you can't see or touch a single one of them. Little surprise, then, that our relationship to time becomes a "subjective phenomenon," as Jay Allison puts it. "There can be interminable minutes and there can be years that go by in the blink of an eye."

As a radio producer, however, Jay has learned to precisely measure time so that interviews fit in their allotted segments. I encourage you to do the same. When we claim time's absence ("no time") or set ourselves to "making" time, we unnecessarily inflate our perception of its scarcity. We also set ourselves to a stress-inducing activity, fighting with reality.

If you haven't already, begin to relate to time from an empowering perspective. Focus on the only factor you can truly control: your choice as to how you use the time you have.

Revising your time-talk

Time Is – period

When your self-talk about a specific interval of minutes or hours veers toward *too little, too much,* or *none,* revise it to: *[Time interval] is [repeat],* or "Ten minutes is ten minutes." Accepting a period of time as a simple reality allows us to step back, much as a sculptor does with a stone, and pose the empowering question, *How can I best use this?*

A similar sense of control can be found in an affirmation Sarah shared with me: "I always have plenty of time for myself, my family, my work in the world and to have fun." Each of Sarah's pursuits will occur because she has empowered herself to use her time in the ways that are important to her.

Own the overflow

Most of us have at some point distractedly poured a beverage so that it overflows a glass. When that occurs, we don't tend to ascribe the overflow to the glass' size. Rather, we recognize our lack of attention. When it comes to pouring too much into a container of time, however, we are often less forthright about our responsibility. Our self-talk tends to put the blame on time – and that does nothing to help us feel masterful. When we toss off phrases like "too short on time" instead of "I didn't prioritize," we pass up the opportunity to take charge of what time there is.

Remodeling the time you have

Like the cabinets or closets in your home that help to both contain your belongings and free up your space, certain slowlutions will help reshape your "time-space."

Recalibrate your sense of time

While some people seem to naturally have a precise sense of time, many struggle to realistically predict the hours or minutes needed for the accomplishment of their tasks.

To build mastery in this area, begin to take note of how long recurring tasks and errands take – *without rushing*. The next 3 times you do these activities at a comfortable pace, chart their durations. Then, total the times for each and divide by 3. Use the resulting averages to more accurately schedule your day.

For example:

Recurring Task	Hours / Minutes	Average Time
Weekly grocery shopping	44, 62, 59	55 mins.
Monthly budget report	3:10, 3:00, 3:08	3 hrs. 6 mins.
Daily commute	32, 26, 30	29 mins.

Such a chart, while tedious to complete, will be eye-opening as to how someone's hasty pace can develop. After all, who wouldn't hurry when trying to complete in 44 minutes what, on average, takes 55? This recalibration of tasks to time will also help you piece together the number of activities that can fit within any time-period. For instance, if the "charter" above was at the office at 2 p.m. and needed to be home by 6 p.m., would a 4-hour period really be sufficient to prepare the monthly budget report, travel to the grocery, shop, and get home? The figures above suggest that it wouldn't be.

With such information at hand, you will provide yourself realistic choices that won't result in increasing your pace or tense activation – as long as you reassure yourself that what you don't get done today *will* still get done. The shortage of time in our example might, perhaps, prompt you to cut several items off your shopping list or to check whether the report really needs to be turned in the next day. If everything does need doing, you might pick up the phone and ask for help buying the groceries.

Ask for help: When time is limited and we need to ask for help in order to bolster our resources, we often judge ourselves as inadequate rather than resourceful. Yet, the cultivation of balance requires that we interweave receiving with giving. As you ask for help, it may help to remind yourself that you've helped others, and will again. As well, think of your request as not an imposition, but an opportunity for the other person: perhaps, for example, they'll feel good about giving you a hand, or they'll learn something through doing so.

Reshaping Time

- Recalibrate your sense of time
- Ask for help
- Say No
- Let go of perfection
- Simplify & prioritize
- Love what speedstress hates
- Treat deadlines as suspect

Say No: Few of us would expect an experienced gardener who lives in deer country to grow vegetables in an unfenced plot. Offer yourself the same kindness and common sense. *No* is the verbal equivalent of a fence-line: It helps safeguard what's most important to the speaker, and keeps unwelcome distractions at bay. So, when you string a *No* between yourself and someone else's request, remind yourself that you're doing so in order to slow down and keep your energy and tension within helpful bounds. Each restorative *No* will move you closer to your next heartfelt *Yes*.

You may want to soften your response with phrasing such as *I'm so sorry, but I can't ... Maybe another time*. If you find yourself especially challenged at turning someone down, make a habit of responding with a "place holder" such as *Let me sleep on that* or *I need to think about that*. You don't owe anyone an explanation as to why. Use the additional time to ask yourself some of the questions Sarah shares, "Do I want to do this? Does it fit easily in my time schedule or will I have to juggle to fit it in? Is this really an important thing for me to do?"

Let go of perfection: Perfection is like a mirage in the desert … we keep moving toward it − and never quite get there. If that isn't a trigger for speedstress, I don't know what is! As human beings, we are complex and fallible beings living in the midst of complicated and demanding circumstances. So, begin to question the time-consuming quest for what's unattainable. I encourage you to evaluate your plans to complete tasks *within the context* of both their absolute necessity and your present resources and circumstances.

Simplify & prioritize your to-dos: When making decisions, a Mexican tycoon who has business interests across the globe tries to limit the factors he weighs to those that fit on one piece of paper. Set yourself up for similar success with your task-list. Kevin Webb recommends making sure "you've got a good match between your goals and your resources." As much as you can, limit the items on your daily list to what *must* and *can* be completed *without forsaking slowing down*; then, note them down in order of importance. Trust that you'll complete the remaining items as it becomes necessary or timely to do so. You can safely assume that some of the less pressing to-dos will naturally recede from your list with time or with a shift in your thinking. Simplifying and prioritizing will help you stop feeling like your to-dos are *doing you in*. Says Sarah of this only-the-necessary approach, "I do this on a day to day basis and the results are lovely."

Treat deadlines as suspect: Our speedstressed world is rife with false deadlines that arise from, as someone once told me, "5-minute decisions." Sometimes we set those deadlines, and sometimes others do; either way, if making an upcoming deadline is stress-inducing, slip on your detective's hat and put the target date to the test:

• Consider its source and its finality.

- Are other contributors to the project in line to meet the date – or not?
- Assess the benefits and the downsides of extending the deadline.
- What are the most likely ramifications of asking whether the date can be extended?

If, after all your inquiry, the deadline is unshaken, put its certainty to use for you: Offer it as the reason you need to put something else on the back burner. None of us can do it all – and especially not at the same time!

Love what speedstress hates: Traffic jams, lines, delays, and similar circumstances are not, as we can so easily feel when speedstressed, signs that the world is conspiring against us. They are simply part of the rhythm of life. And, while you can't do a thing about their existence, you can do a lot with your thinking. Recognize these moments as the unexpected, free time-space that they are. Take a deep breath; practice *i slow*. You can't get to where you're going when you wanted to, but you can arrive in a happier and calmer frame of mind.

What's my slowlution?

≋ In especially tense circumstances, shift your focus in order to identify real positives, whether rewards, resources, or new opportunities.

≋ When you've assessed that a to-do is outsized for your time, widen your thinking, instead of picking up your pace. What part of the task can be postponed? Can you ask for help or strategize a more efficient way to handle it?

Chapter 18

This, Too, Shall Pass:
Relating Anew to Anxiety

"It is awfully hard work doing nothing."

~ Oscar Wilde

Anxiety will prove the truth of Mr. Wilde's words as you first slow down.

Because the brain equates unfamiliarity with lack of safety, slowing your habitual hasty pace will spark anxiety in you. Sharon Dornberg-Lee discovered just that as she intentionally began to take walks and reserve time for lunch. "[The fact] I have even less time to focus on work in some ways creates more anxiety, but I find it's more than worth it," she says.

Sharon has learned to co-exist with her anxiety, rather than resisting it or letting it block her from moving toward calmer energy. As a means to the same end, we'll explore anxiety as your ally, and your relationship to it through the lenses of resistance, acceptance, and what I call "conscious co-existence." Relating in new ways to your in-the-body experience of the feeling will complement your efforts to decelerate your thinking.

Anxiety as ally

As a start, let me introduce what may seem a counter-intuitive idea: Anxiety, though it can be misguided at times, is on your side. I say this because the emotion's sole purpose is to keep you safe. Its unsettling, uncomfortable nature exists for a reason, prodding our minds to alertly scan the environment for threat and priming our bodies to spring into "fight or flight."

Because our felt experience of the emotion is, at best, unsettling and, often, distressing, we usually don't respond to its protective intent with anything close to gratitude. As a result, rather than assessing whether anxiety's "Danger!" signal is accurate, we sometimes perceive our less-than-comfortable experience of the feeling as the threat itself. We may try to escape or resist anxiety, whether by eating, drinking or, as we've seen, by staying overly busy. Thus, the anxiety that will arise as you slow down may prove an especially strong potential trigger for the hasty behaviors you are trying to change.

Resistance, however, is futile.

Resistance

Resistance of any emotion can take many forms. We may try, consciously or not, to repress a feeling through drinking or eating. Regret or self-judgment about being in the grip of a difficult emotion can also serve as a way to fight it. As we've seen, haste and overdoing can also serve as a form of resistance, temporarily blocking one's experience of anxiety.

Resisting doesn't work for long, however.

There's a reason for this: Resistance imbues what it resists with energy. As illustration, find something hard and round – a small exercise ball or object – to put in the palm of your hand. Hold your palm open and notice your experience of what's in your hand. Next, close your fist and try to crush the ball or object. This intensifies your experience of it, doesn't it?

You've likely experienced this phenomenon during instances of interpersonal resistance (more commonly known as arguing!). One voice rises and so, then, does the other; one accusation elicits another. Each person, by resisting the other, sends attention and energy toward him or her. Until one party breaks away, the arguers are bound together. They are, in other words, attached (negatively) to the very person they are resisting! How could this paradox not occur? The specific nature of resistance means that it exists only in relation to what is resisted.

The futility of resistance is only magnified when we apply it to our feelings. As embodied energy, they are not only in us, they are *of* us. So, when we judge or resist our feelings, we are resisting ourselves! Trying to outrun or negate part of who we are is not only impossible, it's draining.

We can't outpace ourselves, nor can we ever do away with emotions. Emotions are energy; as such, they shift rather than die. Our feelings rise, peak and decline, and, then, their energy transitions into yet another emotion. When we're in the grip of anxiety, however, it's easy to forget that our in-the-body experience of it will pass.

Because the potential to become anxious will exist through every moment of your life, learning to coexist with your unease will serve you well. To that end, let David Greenberger inspire you. Like many artists, David is rarely sure how his next creation will manifest. He's realized, over time, that a feeling of strong anxiety, even panic, about his lack of clarity can help "redirect" his work. "I think a sense of panic is really one of the ways in which we edit and take stock," says David.

David has learned to accept his anxiety; he treats it like an ally. I encourage you to do the same.

Acceptance

Acceptance does not mean that we enjoy anxiety or that we comply with its every urge to action. Far from it! Rather, we learn to accept its presence and recognize its limitations, as well as its good intentions. Anxiety is an emotion – and just that. It derives from the brain, but *it* doesn't have one. Rather, anxiety offers an embodied experience that warns us about *possible* risks, threats and danger, and prompts us toward action. The feeling itself, however, offers no factual or evidentiary information about whether the threat is real or action is appropriate. Our reasoning mind must make that call.

A bit of background will serve as a good place to start the acceptance process.

You'll have noticed that I previously described anxiety as "misguided at times." That's because the area of the brain that governs our fear response, the amygdala, developed many millennia ago, when dangers were usually clear and, often, life-threatening. As a result, anxiety prompts us to react, rather than think.

Threat ⟶ Anxiety/Fear ⟶ Urge to Action ⟶ Action!

Stelle's description of her experience while slowing down illustrates how easily anxiety can work us up into a reactive state.

"My brain starts worrying," she says. 'What am I not doing that I should be doing? I can't keep this up. I won't be getting clients. I won't be getting work done, and I should be worried about money, and I should be worried about not having enough work'."

These reactions are entirely understandable. We all have things we need to do, including making a living. Yet, we often don't recognize how our anxiety, simplistic warning system that it is, exaggerates the possibility of negative outcomes from slowing down, and overlooks its benefits. In Stelle's situation, how helpful would returning to work have been? We, who are calm in this moment, can easily see that a few minutes of downtime would not throw Stelle into poverty; in fact, that period of rest or recreation might do a good deal to calm and recharge her.

Had Stelle identified her thoughts as anxious and overblown, she would have been able to limit their impact. Similarly, the sooner you recognize that you're anxious, the sooner you can accept the feeling and begin to relate to it differently.

Recognizing your anxiety

Emotions are elusive and ever-changing. They arise, stimulated by any number of experiences - thoughts, memories, activities, or physical postures and sensations - and they recede on their own timetable. Consequently, anxiety – or any emotion - will not be present in one moment and, in the next, it will be; that doesn't mean, however, that you will instantly become aware of it. If you've been habitually *speed*stressed, you may be so used to feeling anxiety that you may not notice its increase as you first practice *i slow* – with the result that worry about what you're not getting done hijacks you back into hurrying. So, it's important to become more attuned to how you experience anxiety. Only then can you relate to it more promptly and effectively.

Next time you recognize that you're anxious, become the gentle detective. Turn your awareness to your experience, re-minding yourself that there is no right or wrong about either the feeling or how you experience it. Apply a close inner eye, noting briefly how your anxiety is manifesting in your sensations and thoughts. For example, you might remark … *breathing fast … a "dire outcomes" thought … jaw tight … worrying about …* and so on.

Just as you watch the ever-changing surf while visiting the beach, track how your experience of anxiety shifts – or doesn't. Does it lodge in one part of your body or move around? What does anxiety make you want to do – for example, flee back into work, thrum your fingers, or take sips of water? Your *s-step* scans will prove invaluable in helping you recognize what happens in body and mind.

Acceptance can be cultivated by acknowledging, *O.K., I'm anxious about slowing down. I don't enjoy this feeling, but I knew it would be here at first. How can I most helpfully relate to my unease?* This stance sets the stage for consciously co-existing with anxiety.

Conscious co-existence

In order to co-exist with a feeling, we need to move from accepting its presence to consciously shifting our position in *relation* to it. Doing so will prove far more effective than trying to resist the emotion itself. Anxiety, no less than ocean surf, will change and recede, but none of us are in charge of when that happens. We are in charge, however, of relating to it in a way that doesn't shoot reinforcing energy its way.

Now, what exactly do I mean by 'shifting your position' to an experience of anxiety? Clinical psychologist Karen Kingsolver's experience after she suffered an eye hemorrhage will help answer that question. "Everything went kind of dark and quiet. Suddenly I couldn't drive. I was taken out of my hubbub busy life from one day to the next." For the self-described "projects girl" there was now only "severe pain, and the quiet and the fear."

Healing from eye surgery prohibited any type of movement: Karen had to lie face down and remain absolutely still, no small challenge for a woman whose "primary way of coping with anything … was to try very, very hard to push myself."

Karen had little choice but to learn to co-exist with her pain and fear – and she did so in a very wise manner. She didn't deny her distress; rather, she intentionally listened to "healing sounds." Doing so widened her awareness out from its pinpoint focus on her extreme discomfort, lessening the intensity of her experience.

Unlike Karen, when slowing down makes you anxious, you'll have the option to swing back into a hasty task-focus. To lessen the chance of doing that, consider some soothing or enjoyable ways to co-exist with your unease:

- Use a *soothing slowlution* – not in order to get rid of the anxiety, but to expand your awareness out from it, as Karen did. Breathe in and out slowly; recall a peaceful image or memory. Offer yourself kindness.

- *Release some of anxiety's energy* by shifting into a "fast" enjoyable slowlution.

- *Rate (1-10) the shifting intensity* of the feeling as it migrates through your body.

- Create an enjoyable *distraction*: go to a movie, call a friend, cook a nice meal. Keep reminding yourself that the anxiety will pass.

- Use helpful *affirmations*; for example: *In this moment, I'm uncomfortable but safe.*

In this modern era, our "threats" are often complex and ambiguous; yet, they rarely put our lives at risk. As a result, co-existing with anxiety will also require that you reframe its felt urgency by calling on reason.

Calling on reason

As you come to know your anxiety better, you'll find that your experience of it becomes less rattling. This makes sense: You're co-existing with the feeling, rather than resisting and energizing it. As a result, you'll be better able to access calmer, reasoned thinking. This is no small development because, when you're employing reason, you're by definition no longer 100 percent in your emotional experience. With your reason a bit more in charge, as diagrammed below, you can choose to think through, rather than succumb to, your anxiety's habitual urge to action: *Hurry! Get busy!*

Slow down ⟶ Anxiety/fear ⟶ Urge to action ⟶
<u>Call on reason/Assess</u> ⟶ Continue slowing down,
in most cases

Reasoning through your response to anxiety

Assess anxiety's urge to action: Anxiety's urge is usually nothing more than an energy that needs evaluating. Explore whether resuming tasks or picking up your pace is really warranted. A feeling of danger doesn't mean that danger is actually present; yet, it's all too easy to fall into the brainless short-circuit of emotional "reasoning:" *If I'm anxious that means there's something to be anxious about.* And, off we go, on the run again.

Trust your ability to be sensible: Check in with yourself: Are you taking small, reasonable steps to slow down? If so, reassure yourself that you are slowing down in a way that won't compromise you.

Normalize your anxiety: Tell yourself, *This was predictable. Anxiety pops up during habit change.* Would you expect someone who is trying to give up sweets not to feel uneasy when offered a slice of cake? Give yourself the same understanding.

Reframe: See your anxiety as a positive sign that you are doing what you set out to do: Change your speedstress habit.

Say "this, too, shall pass": Remind yourself that intense anxiety won't last forever. Like an ocean wave, the feeling will shift and dissipate.

Return to sender: You may receive a variety of reactions when and if you mention that you're working on slowing down. Some feedback will be supportive, but some will be discouraging or, even, anxiety-provoking. When this happens, send the message back; don't take it in. Instead, do the following in your mind:

Picture yourself as a martial artist standing still, feet firmly braced on the floor. Raise your hands in front of your chest, palms outward. Let your non-dominant hand remain still, while your dominant hand gently but firmly pushes the unhelpful message away from you.

Wish the other person no ill will; you are simply returning their opinion to them.

Slow down _despite_ your anxiety. Learning to co-exist with your jitters is the only way to move beyond them.

What's my slowlution?

🥀 Begin to pay attention to the physical or mental signs that you're anxious. Work with the tools in this chapter.

🥀 What simple language could you use to greet your anxiety as neutrally and realistically as possible?

Composed Life Press
Durham, NC

Dear Reader,

Thank you so much for your interest in ***Slowing Down in a Speedstressed World***. I sincerely hope that the book's been of assistance to you.

As an author who is self-publishing, I am – appropriately! - practicing slow-marketing. My marketing staff consists of myself – *and* as many enthusiastic and willing readers as possible. Consequently, getting the word out about this book depends on 3 resources only:

1. The book's quality
2. My marketing efforts
   &
3. The "people-power" of appreciative readers.

I hope that you're one of those readers, who will spread the word about slowing down and about this book.

If you benefitted from these pages, I will be so grateful if you do at least 1 of the following:

1. Tell others about the book; lend it or gift it.
2. Tweet about it/follow me at **@slowlutions**
3. "Like" the book & my website **www.slowlutions.com** on Facebook
4. Write a review on Amazon or other sites
5. Ask your local bookstore or your book club to order the book
6. Post the book's cover on Instagram or other sites
7. Email a review to me to post on my website **www.slowlutions.com**

You can easily share about the book through my website **www.slowlutions.com**.

Whatever you choose, please do it slowly and feel good about helping others to slow down. In fact, consider yourself a slowlution!

Thanks very much,

~~Marian~~ *Marian*

www.slowlutions.com

Specific Slowlutions

Chapter 19

In Plain Sight:
Slowing Down at Work

"Sooner or later ... you have to give yourself credit for knowing what's true for you and you have to act on it."

~ Rhonda Miller

From the morning mist over a lake in Golden Gate Park a tableau emerges: Arms and legs seem to float in the air as the torsos of Asian elders turn slowly, impelled as if by no more than a puff of breath. Breathe, turn, breathe, step, balance. Tai chi's silent, calm movements seem to waft through the air to near-by commuters, making it easy to imagine their goals and demands suspended even as their buses whine down Fulton Street toward the business district.

You can practice *i slow* on the job with the silence and subtlety of an ancient martial art. Many slowlutions can be enacted in plain sight of others without them being the wiser. If one seems noticeable, ask yourself Am I going to get fired for [slowlution]? For example, *Am I going to get fired for walking more slowly, with focus, to the bathroom?* That query seems tinged with absurdity, doesn't it? (Obviously, if the answer is *Yes*, don't do it.)

Your body, moods, and energy are part of your work process; you can't remove them, as you do your coat, before settling in to the business of the day. The cultivation of a calmer mood and a more energized body and mind will help your work, as Sally Starrfield discovered after she had the chance to compare a speedstressed educational work environment with a calmer one. "Slowing down allows you to balance and center, to observe others and not just react to all the stimuli," she says. "You're more productive and find more satisfaction in your work."

Your *o-step* simply needs to be appropriate to the work environment so as not to cause you more stress! As you read through the ideas below, consider how obvious they would be to others.

Relate anew to your workload

It is not our workload or our time constraints – short of a truly tight deadline - that inhibit us from taking regular discreet breaks. It is not even your boss. True, they may overload you with work or ask for a quick response, but they rarely include in their instructions, *No eating, no bathroom break, no deep breathing*. It is we who issue such commands.

Unless you want to speak up about your workload, accept the reality that, for now, it's too high. Of course, no one *should* be chronically overloaded with responsibilities and, in a fair world, you wouldn't be – but you are. In the midst of this dilemma, your choice, other than looking for another job or trying to institute change in your current one, is to take charge of how you care for yourself. Taking brief moments of ease throughout the day can help you think more clearly and feel more in control. Slowing down, says Mary Bennett, contributes to people "being more considerate in terms of decisions you make at work. Being more courteous and taking time for people."

Set your tone for the day

At the beginning of your work shift, avoid racing into your tasks. That will only send your psyche a message of *I'm behind* before you've even begun. Slowly hang up your coat; make a point of greeting at least one person. Remind yourself that regularly slowing down from speedstress will benefit your work, that you're still employed despite perpetually feeling behind on meeting your goals.

Set the tone for your workday - that choice is always yours. Consider the next eight hours a clean slate. You have no ability to reach back into the previous day; your influence rests solely in the current moment. Consequently, think about each task as off to a fresh start today, rather than behind schedule from yesterday. Doing so will help you feel more in control.

If you're unclear on some aspect of the day's tasks, or your position in relation to them, get more information. "Stress isn't necessarily tied to the amount of work, or even the number of hours," says CEO Joe Colopy. "It really often is tied more to if people are uncomfortable in their positions or there is uncertainty."

It's also important to acknowledge that unexpected events may create a sudden change in your plans. So, remind yourself that what your boss or another department decides is often beyond your control. You'll do the best you can, but it won't be perfect or, perhaps, even complete on that day.

As you continue setting the tone for your day, stay rooted in yourself – breathe and notice the feel of your body in the chair. Remind yourself that calm thinking is needed if you are to work smarter, rather than faster. "If you go slower," notes Sally, "you can recognize more how to prioritize what really needs to be done versus what someone's asking you, or what you're assuming someone else wants you to do."

Pitch a Calmer Day

If your boss throws you a counter-productive curve ball as a morning greeting, or dumps an impossible amount of work in your lap, prepare a logical argument for a more realistic plan. Then present it – skillfully.

- First, acknowledge the items that your boss has already described as priorities. Agree with what you can.

- Propose your changes, emphasizing your desire to work as efficiently and productively as possible. Share any information you've got about the importance of certain tasks, the availability of resources, and so on.

- Remind your boss of what else you have on your plate. Do so matter-of-factly rather than in a negative or whining manner.

- Describe how your plan will benefit your – and, by extension, your boss' - work process and goals.

Work smarter!

- Take breaks; make calm your mantra.

- Prioritize/organize.

- Check email only every half-hour, if allowed.

- Prevent duplication of efforts: Coordinate with others.

- Delegate, if possible.

- Offer work conversations full attention.

- Ask yourself: What efficiency am I not thinking of?

- Challenge unrealistic or false deadlines with facts.

- Before putting unfinished tasks aside, affix "next step" notes to them.

If your boss agrees, great. In that case, reward yourself by noting how your choice for a slower

Slowlutions kit

For greater calm ...

Relaxing scents, music; favorite poems, massage oil, vacation pictures, lavender sachet, a textured ball, inspiring sayings, shells and other reminders of nature ...

To energize ...

A list of desk exercises and stretches, jokes, photos of fun times, reminders to get up and move ...

To motivate i slow practice ...

Statistics about stress' effect on work and health, reminders to practice, your family's picture, a count of completed *i slows*, a loved one's comment ...

start to the day has resulted in positive, practical changes. Notice the effect on your sense of control or well-being.

If your boss doesn't budge on her priorities, or doesn't even hear you through, congratulations are still in order. You slowed down in order to plan smarter, and you've shared suggestions. Your boss didn't agree, but that doesn't mean she may not begin to notice that your ideas make sense over time. Be sure to notice any positive results that did occur. Did thinking things through help you, for example, anticipate a few roadblocks or find a few short cuts through the day's work?

Resolve to do the best you can. Remind yourself that you can't do everything; that, plain and simple, is reality.

Create a slowlutions kit

Because so little in the work environment supports – or cues - slowing down, we need to import what does. To help "grow your slow," create a slowlutions kit – perhaps a small basket, box or bag – that contains items you can use for breaks. Keep it out on your desk or in a drawer you open frequently.

Any items that help you to relax, energize, or widen your focus from tasks belong in your kit. If you're having a hard time allowing yourself to take a break, include motivating reminders to do so.

Where possible, extend your kit into your workspace. Put up a photo of someone doing jumping jacks. Does a windowless space make your energy harder to calm? A poster of an empty armchair next to a sparkling bay calmed my senses in a closet-like office. You might dress in looser, softer clothes that whisper kindness rather than *push, push, push.*

Of course, the best part of your slowlutions kit is you. Indeed, each of us is a complete kit in and of ourselves. Our memory, imagination, body and thoughts travel with us wherever we go, as does the choice to employ them. Whether in a bare room or in an office jam-packed with equipment and people, we can always make the decision to, as Sarah writes, "Stop to take a few slow, deep breaths."

Walk slowly

When was the last time someone came up to you and commented on your pace as you walked around the office? *Exactly.*

Walking slowly with focus is a powerful method for slowing down in plain sight.

Moving more slowly brings you back from your speed-stressed tilt towards *Next!*, allowing your awareness to align with your body, Rushing does just the opposite. "When the thought of my movement and the movement of my body aren't even connected," says Zelda Lockhart, "I'm moving based on a thought that I had five minutes ago, but I'm already thinking the next thing, that means that my body and mind are not in synch and I'm more likely to fall down or bump into something."

As you practice a slower pace, notice the grounding feel of your feet on the floor, how your activation level immediately declines. Slow your breath to your pace.

When you notice yourself speeding up, tell yourself kindly, *There's no need to rush*. Let go of any belief that the time it takes you to go from point A to point B is the 'make or break' factor in getting your work done. It's not.

Eat lunch

I risk mentioning the obvious only because of its importance. When our food consumption goes off schedule, our body's normal cycles become confused, resulting in a state of physiological stress. Taking time to slowly eat a meal will not only move you toward calm, it will boost your energy. If you find yourself resisting, re-read the chapter on the body's delicate and intertwined processes. Challenge yourself: Would you, for instance, send an elderly person who is shaky on his feet outside without his walker? Of course not! Offer yourself the same consideration. Our bodies become shaky without regular refueling, as does our ability to work effectively. If you share lunch with others, their support may also serve to lessen your stress.

"Workable" slowlutions

*Always remember …
You are the person
most in charge
of how you move
through your day.*

Take in the view at a window.

Offer someone a compliment; chat for a minute or two.

Ask for, and offer, help.

Massage your hands as you put on lotion; breathe deeply.

End your day by relaxing into your chair for a few minutes.

Take greater note of what you did get done than what you didn't.

Put the 'rest' back into restroom

As my friend entered his work restroom, he heard the familiar taps of keystrokes coming from a bathroom stall. Recounting this, Jerry shrugged ruefully. "You gotta stay connected," he said.

The unidentified tapper was missing an important point: A work restroom is an ever-present haven for slowing down. So, help the room live up to its name.

Let's state the obvious, however: Often, work restrooms can be pretty unappealing. Yours may have dirty paint, gray soap smudges in the sinks, torn flyers dangling from stall doors. Doors may bang and toilets will flush. People enter; they may even linger to gripe about their stress – just as you are hoping to ease yours.

This is all challenging, of course, to one's focus, but also helpful for retraining it. As you sit on the toilet, let closed eyes and inner focus morph your stall into a snug place of safety. The small rectangular space can become a container for a range of slowlutions: visualization, meditation, happy anticipation or memories.

Focus on the firmness of the toilet lid against your bottom, the floor beneath your feet. If the door were a blank screen, what soothing image would you project there? Expanding your definition of restroom supplies may also help: Take a puzzle, your i-pod, or a poem into your stall.

As distractions arise, refocus on slowing down, or work them into the process. Let a flushing sound invite the image of a fountain. Sweep overheard comments away from you with a gentle inner martial art move; imagine them floating away like feathers.

Wash your hands with focus, enjoying the water's warmth and walk slowly back to your workstation. Notice the difference between how you feel now and how you would have felt had you dashed into and out of the restroom.

Transform to-dos into slow-dos

At times, stopping work in order to briefly rest or re-energize with full focus will truly not be possible. Take hope, though: Integrating slowlutions into your flow of work is often possible – and effective. For instance, straightening up your desk or office slowly and with focus makes a wonderful "slow-do." Be cautious, though, as to how frequently you use this type of slow-down. Speedstressed thinking about never needing to put tasks aside can easily set you on a path back into haste and habit.

Slower typing: Let's imagine putting this "slow-do" into action while typing a document. Rather than typing pell-mell throughout, at the bottom of each page you might decide to stop, take two slow deep breathes, and remember that you exist no less than your work does.

Affirmations: The silent repetition of an affirmation can serve as a wonderful slowlution as you work. If you're like many people, however, you may characterize affirmations as uncomfortably "touchie-feelie." I encourage you to reframe them as statements that can, with repetition, morph into useful beliefs and behaviors. Many recovering alcoholics have used AA's maxim, "Fake it until you make it" to great effect (referring to practicing the skills of sobriety even as a craving for alcohol tugs inside).

You might want to create your own affirmations based on the "Reality" statements in the Rule/Reality list in Chapter 15.

Check in quickly with a supporter: At some point in your flow of work, take a moment to call or email an ally in slowing down. Let them remind you that you are more than your work.

Enhance your quality of work: When no break is possible, use 'slow downs' that promote the quality, innovation, or productivity of the work at hand and also give you a moment or two of ease. For instance, instead of jumping into an urgent assignment, you might choose to reflect on the best way to fulfill it. When you need to problem-solve, call a friend who makes you laugh – your thinking will broaden. As you walk toward what is sure to be a challenging meeting, take some focused, deep breaths or visualize a positive outcome.

As you can see, these slow-dos invite you to take charge of your experience – despite the fact that you have to keep working.

If your boss doesn't have the ability to put him- or herself in your shoes, as skilled managers do, then you need to be your own good boss, one who helps you rebalance so that you can re-engage with your work. Attend briefly, but regularly, to your stress, energy and other needs. You'll feel more in control, and like you have more to give. That's a very good thing for both you and your workplace. According to a study by the Gallup Organization, engaged employees are not only more productive and innovative, they're also less likely to quit.

What's my slowlution?

◔ Use one or more of this chapter's strategies for slowing down in your workplace over the next week. Watch for rewards.

Chapter 20

Retire – without Re-tiring Yourself

*"It really was important for me not to do anything
for 6 months because ... I realized it wasn't such a bad thing
not to be doing something every minute."*

~ Shelley Beason

Retirement is a process, rather than a point of arrival. "It's just like anything, when you come to an end," Carol Shaw says. "You know you need to start a new path, and what is that path going to be?"

How you relate to yourself in early retirement will shape your direction no less than workdays did your weeks. Use *i slow*, paired with kindness, to help recalibrate from any speedstressed pace developed on the job. The goal is to ease into retirement, to give yourself a chance to define it, rather than letting premature commitments do so.

Postpone making commitments

When Shelley Beason retired she vowed not to take on any recurring obligations for six months. "I was tempted, sorely tempted, a couple of times and I didn't, I held myself to it," she recalled. "And what I discovered in that first six months was what I really enjoy is not having a schedule, not having to be some-where at any time."

In early retirement, make exploring your sudden abundance of free time, and how you relate to it, your first standing commitment. Honor this new phase of your life, and open to what you find is true for you, as Shelley did.

Remodel your remodeling plans

Often, if people have the money to spend, they're tempted to start retirement off with a bang – frequently that of a hammer. This is understandable: It's common to dream about renovating home to match one's new life.

Put Shelley's six-month, no-plan plan into effect before you pick up the phone to get estimates. Have fun with designing, but keep an open mind. As you settle into retirement, your needs may change. For instance, if you discover painting as a new passion, adding a small studio may come to seem more useful than enlarging the den. Or, if more houseguests come to visit now that you're free, you may start to ponder an additional guestroom.

Be realistic: Researching pricing and contractors takes time and effort. Remodeling can be a noisy, dirty, cluttered hassle. Jumping into this will do nothing to help you to take pleasure, or slow down, in your early retirement. So, remodel this new stage of your life before you remodel the house.

Cultivate your shifting identity - carefully

When Carol Shaw found herself outside the workforce, she "didn't know where [her] niche was … there is this gap in identity."

Speedstress' task focus can easily cause us to forget that we were complete and worthwhile at the moment of birth – with nary a work-related accessory in sight! Consequently, if you find yourself reluctant to describe yourself as retired, wonder if you are devaluing yourself. Ask family and friends to tell you how you contribute to their lives.

Remind yourself of *slow*'s varied powers and put them to work, attending to birds at the feeder or a grandchild's story. As you experience the new pacing that retirement makes possible, put the scanning and inner listening skills you've honed practicing *i slow* to work. Notice how you react in new circumstances, what lingers with you afterwards, how much downtime you like in a day. For example, does staying home all day feel relaxing or stressful? Do your reactions change over time? As time unwinds, what new interests or urges arise in you?

You may want to bat around ideas for new ventures with friends. However, unless you need to immediately supplement your income, I recommend not latching on to a plan too quickly. As you settle into a pacing that works for you, the appropriate contours of any new project will become clearer to you.

Slow Dates with ... you!

Schedule dates to ...

Hike ... Visit art venues ... Watch an old movie ... Shoot baskets ... Scrapbook ... Picnic ... Meditate... Create ... Browse at the library ... Swim ... Window-shop ...

Be sure to follow through!

Taking your time to adjust will free you further from the speedstressed extremes and rules that you could easily carry into this new phase of life. Instead of cultivating *Next!*, familiar though it is, cultivate is, *am*, and *now*. As you allow yourself to intentionally attend to and participate in the present moment, your responses over time will guide you to where you need to go next. Even Carol, who was, and is, a doer, is more comfortable with her new life. "I like having some free time," she tells me.

Go on slow dates – with you

Make regular, enjoyable appointments with yourself to slow down. Whether a date to read a book on the sofa or to attend a street fair, these activities will help you structure any day that feels overwhelmingly empty. For ideas, subscribe to community list servs. Talk to friends about interesting and enjoyable experiences they've had locally. Make the search for your next "date" fun: Enjoy the fact that you finally have the time to seek out new adventures!

Afterward, review your experience, just as you would a date with another person. What did you like – or dislike? Did this date give you an idea for another? Take note of your preferences; they may guide later choices.

Stay connected

The first weeks of retirement can make one all too aware of how the bustle and chatter of a workplace filled a need for connection. Friends and family who are still employed may offer you a mirror image of your former pace: They may be less available than you want, or they may be envious of what they imagine as a placid sea of free time. Yet, here you are, with your very human need to connect. Pay attention to it; isolation is not helpful.

Connecting ...

Start a retiree slowing circle.

Make a weekly date with a partner or friend.

Run some errands for friends so they have time to visit.

Fully participate in passing interactions as you shop, wait on line, etc.

Watch for the rewards.

Take grandkids or young friends on outings.

Take classes.

Visit an inviting café or library.

Shelley Beason resolved to reach out to friends from whom she had "drifted apart." She says, "And so now, one of the

169

things I'm doing is I'm trying to rebuild those [relationships]. Fortunately no one that I'm attempting to rebuild a relationship with feels hurt by my lack of attention because they were not attending either."

Make a slowlution out of brainstorming ways to spend time with friends and family, or to simply be around other people. Close your eyes and let your mind wander. Always, remind yourself that you're a part of the human race, no matter your employment status!

Note your accomplishments

Before she retired, Shelley Beason equated not doing with "feeling not productive, like I wasn't contributing, not worthwhile."

Thinking in terms of accomplishments will help you avoid using the employment-centered measure of productivity. For Marcy Litle, this meant confronting "having pretty narrow or unexamined notions about what might be useful."

Accomplishments stand on their own; their worth isn't dependent on doing more of them or doing them faster. Rather, they instill pride and a sense of satisfaction. So, invite yourself to recognize what you do in any day in a new way. If you are tired and you allow yourself to rest, label that an accomplishment: It is. Be sure to notice when you've made a difference in someone's day; an act of kindness is qualitatively different from, for example, meeting quarterly goals, but it's no less important. Even small errands noted as completed can provide one a sense of satisfaction.

The act of appreciation – whether for yourself or others - is an accomplishment in and of itself. Your *w-step* will have attuned you to watch for the rewards of your own actions, but you'll also more easily notice others' positive and attention-worthy acts. Sharing appreciation is a worthy accomplishment in a world where it's too easy to become distracted from doing so. Your feedback is sure to make the other person feel "seen."

Nature and art are also deserving of our appreciative regard. Taking in a beautiful scene or a vibrant piece of art can accomplish many positive things: An increased sense of well-being, a resolve to protect nature, or, perhaps, an interest in taking an art class. Would we call these productive in the way of the work world? Probably not, but that makes them no less valid.

When you struggle with feeling unproductive, ask yourself whether your motivation to get busy arises from a speedstressed push to do. If it does, consider, *What is it I'd like to accomplish today?*

Greet feelings with kindness

With more time and less distraction, you may become more aware of your feelings, and uncomfortably so at times. An increase in slow time may mean for you what Sarah predicts for herself, "I would look inside and I'm afraid of what I might find."

Encountering these uneasy parts of you is an entirely normal part of your journey into retirement. You may feel you're lacking in self-worth as a retiree, or working friends may make comments that leave you feeling guilty for having free time. Old emotional challenges may suddenly make themselves known. Review the chapters on working with anxiety, thoughts, and self-judgment (many of those skills can be used with a range of feelings). Rather than becoming overly busy, treat any challenging inner experiences as you would a guest: Offer kindness and curiosity. Set limits, though: Be sure to balance such exploration with enjoyable activities.

If you begin to feel that distressing emotions are taking charge of you, talk to a wise friend or, if you can afford to, see a psychotherapist. Talking about your emotional experience can help you air it out, providing new perspective. There's no right or wrong way to do retirement, but it should not be about suffering, or feeling alone with your distress.

Set boundaries

Recently I met with a father who was struggling with setting boundaries with an adult daughter in need of a babysitter. The man told me that, while he was concerned for his daughter, he hadn't retired in order to work full-time again.

Beware the well-intentioned reasoning of family and friends: that retirement has turned you into someone with "all the time in the world." This is a frequent and somewhat understandable misconception held by people still in the workforce; yet, it's merely a line drawing of retirement, rather than a full portrait.

There's likely a twofold reality going on here. First, you may be the only person who can attend to your needs, errands, and interests, and they can take up a good deal of time. And yet, it's probably also true that you enjoy helping loved ones, as Shelley Beason does. "What finally convinced me to retire was I wanted to be more available to my family and to my friends," she told me. But remember, she's also the person with the six-month plan. Shelley knows the wisdom of setting boundaries.

Allow yourself to both help others *and* draw the line that preserves your energy and encourages enjoyment of your new life. Commiserate with the person who wants help, and confirm that you will offer future assistance, but in a way and at a time that works for you. Help him or her brainstorm how to find new sources of assistance. There's a real benefit to doing so: Each time your friend reaches out to new resources, his or her world will expand.

Tell yourself, *If I lived hundreds of miles away, they'd have to – and would – figure out other solutions.* Encourage mental distance by remembering that you are but one person in a town of potential helpers. If you feel guilty, try shifting into a more appropriate and compassionate response. For example, rather than beating yourself up, recall that you were in their place at one time. This is your time to both help *and* slow down.

Setting boundaries not only helps us stay rested and refreshed, it is an act of self-respect, as well as a way to value what we do say *Yes* to. "I never said No to anything," says Carol Shaw. "I get it now – finally – that you can't do everything and do it well."

Recognize the help you do offer, and feel good about it.

Take a trip

Travel sparks us, whether the journey takes half a day or a night's flight. Unfamiliar sights, tastes, or customs open us to new possibilities, causing our old frames of reference to tilt. I can think of little better way to lift yourself out of the accustomed and encourage your internal shift from the workplace. Travel not only removes one from the danger of over-committing in our regular environs, it often delivers us to new passions.

The British author, George Sitwell, succumbing to a need to rest after intense over-work, took himself to Italy. He visited more than 200 of Italy's finest gardens – and did nothing. Aptly

173

named, Mr. Sitwell simply sat. He felt the breeze on his cheek, observed the paths and hedges, and the blooms as sunlight and shade fell across them. Out of this time of alert rest emerged *On the Making of Gardens*, a gardening classic of the early 20th century.

Not all of us can travel far and wide, of course, or even want to. Luckily, there are often many ways to shift out of accustomed routines and locales without packing even an overnight bag. What places in your hometown have you not explored - perhaps, a museum or a park? Call up someone you would like to know better and suggest a stroll or meal in a novel setting. Drive out in the country, or into the city, or let language carry you to a faraway place as you join a foreign language conversation club.

As you "travel" out of your old context, what strikes you? With time and attention, those experiences will weave into your new narrative, one you might title *On the Making of My Retirement*.

Make friends with being

Stillness, silence, being - they can hum with energy and vitality when we slow down to experience them. Soon after leaving work, however, it can prove difficult to settle down in that way. "I was talking with a friend yesterday about how ingrained in my body being sort of tensed up and alert is," says Marcy Litle, "and how much it interferes with being and presence."

Letting yourself simply be - whether that means scanning your unfolding sensations or overlooking a beautiful scene with your feet up - can offer unexpected benefits. "When I slow down and when I get still and I get quiet there's another impulse and intuition that's … about a different type of experiencing at a real subtle level," says Dominique Davis.

Becoming comfortable with stillness and quiet takes time. Meditation or yoga can be helpful entryways into being with oneself. If those don't appeal, let yourself become quiet and relaxed on your bed or sofa. Sink into your body; feel how it contacts the surface beneath it. Keep returning to this grounding of 'body meeting surface' as other experiences arise: thoughts, emotions; perhaps, a rumble in your belly occurs or a solution to a niggling problem arises. Don't attach to any of them; keep re-grounding in your contact with the surface beneath you. Or, use your breath as your point of grounding. Focus, and refocus, on it. Let being be all the doing there is.

In retirement, slow down and offer yourself kindness. If you remain open to your experience and approach life with curiosity, your next steps will emerge.

What's my slowlution?

⬱ What practice in this chapter spoke to you? Put it to use.

⬱ Interview some people who have been "practicing" retirement for a while. What helped them? What pitfalls might you want to avoid?

Chapter 21

Slowing Down to Become More Hirable

"You never know where you're going to find an opportunity."

~ Nancy Rimes

Rhonda Miller will help us begin the journey toward a calmer, more effective job search. We find her making her way home after a long-distance visit to friends, sitting in her car at a crossroad. "I don't have to be back for anything," she realized, flabbergasted.

Recently laid off after years of meeting reporting deadlines, Rhonda suddenly recalled that friends lived close by the intersection. She pulled over and called them. "I said, 'OK, I'm turning right.' ... I don't remember a time where I could be at an intersection of a road and decide that I'm going to go this [other] way for a couple of more days."

Speedstress' *morefaster* ethos can obscure an abundance of other turns we might take. Whether you were laid off, fired, or are between jobs for other reasons, slowing down continues to have a high degree of relevance. You may still be moving at your old workplace's harried rhythms; or, your anxiety about finding work may be goading you into a pace that adds an unneeded layer of emotional and interpersonal stress.

Some people, however, experience quite the opposite effect: They become so deactivated that they don't look for work or don't lighten that process through socializing and pursuing interests. Stephen Syta reveled in staying busy as an entrepreneur. However, when his real estate development work faded with the recession, he found himself "sitting around the house." Stephen thought about pursuing some interests, but that's all; he took no action. "I could never really get the motivation to do it because I never really felt like I had a sort of purpose," he says. For people like Stephen, energizing slowlutions can be highly effective in jumpstarting one's day.

Seeking work calls on skills such as organization, creative thought, calm action under stressful circumstances, emotionally-intelligent interactions, and – not least - the willingness to get out of bed each morning and show up. As we've seen, you can support all these attributes by regularly slowing down. Enjoyable, relaxing ways to slow down will help to lessen stress and, as research shows, broaden your thinking. "If you expand the mind, then it expands opportunities, it expands vision," says Dominique Davis based on her time between jobs.

When you're unemployed, wider vision is no small thing. It can affect how you redefine your talents and work experiences, think about networking, or consider your financial options.

Following we'll look at how slowing down can help you frame and manage your time of unemployment, as well as look for work more effectively.

Define your daily purpose

When Carol Shaw's job at a pharmaceutical company was made redundant, she felt adrift. "I worked my whole life," she recalls, "I'd never *not* worked." Unoccupied hours caused her great anxiety. "I should be earning money. That's how my value is determined," Carol thought to herself.

Without the purpose her job imposed, Carol, like many involuntarily dislodged from their employment, felt lost. What was she to do? Who was she?

Slowlutions

- Define your daily purpose
- Create structure
- Revel in your enduring riches
- De-stress the topic of money
- Consider the high cost of rushing
- Slow down for success in interviews

Luckily, you don't have to have all the long-term answers. However, defining your purpose soon after you become unemployed will prove essential to helping you stay positive. Several goals may be applicable:

Finding work: Of course, your primary goal right now is securing a new position. However, shame about being unemployed can get in the way of valuing this entirely honorable endeavor. Consequently, I encourage you to define your employment search as nothing less than your new job because that's exactly what it is. In fact, your new "position" as a job-seeker requires time, focus, steady effort, and interaction with others – all qualities needed to successfully navigate a traditional job.

Spend an *o-step* envisioning a day in which you confidently and productively go about your search. What will you do? What self-talk would be helpful? How do you want to relate to any anxiety? Whom do you want to contact? Rehearse your day, and then put it into practice. Doing so will increase your sense of purpose and motivation.

Exploring a career change: If you have the financial where-withal, and you're fairly certain you'd like to pursue a new line of employment, put your slowing down skills to work: Manage your anxiety so that you can slow your job search down enough to explore new occupations. Go on informational interviews; research up-and-coming employment trends. Remembering what you loved to do as a child can not only prove a relaxing slowlution, it may provide clues you'll want to pursue as you consider a new line of work.

Personal purpose: If you have the time, energy and money to pursue some enjoyable goals, do so. After all, your life is about far more than finding work. Perhaps, you want to take more frequent trips to see your aging parents or you want to take advantage of free time to begin a creative project. Identifying and tackling long-delayed home projects can provide a sense of mastery that carries over to one's job search.

Whatever purposes you define, write them down and look at them at the start of each day. "When we first wake up in the morning," says Keith Spring, "the first thing that happens is there's this instantaneous kind of re-assimilation, 'Now, who am I again? Where am I? What am I doing?'"

Defining your purpose clearly will provide you with ready answers.

Create structure

Daniel Scheck's early response to newly abundant time was one many job seekers have. "I would spend a lot time just wondering what I was going to do with myself for the day, and I still do sometimes," he says. "I find ways to kill time but I feel like I'm not really using my days productively."

Unemployment brings with it an unnerving loss of structure. For many of us, knowing the outline of our day can be calming.

So, in order to lessen the sense of lack of control that can accompany unemployment, structure your days as a first step to fulfilling your purpose.

Stick to fundamentals: Get up at your usual weekday time, make the bed, get dressed, and eat breakfast. Next, sit down and set some purpose-driven goals for the day. Taking into account time for meals, household needs, and slow time, list the number of goal-related tasks that you can likely accomplish moving at a calm pace.

It's also helpful to set weekly goals that you work towards between Monday and Friday. For instance, how many networking appointments do you want to go to? How many hours of research? When you don't follow-through, kindly explore why.

Remember the importance of rewards: Congratulate yourself for what you do get done, rather than focusing on what's yet undone. Switch unmet goals to a fresh list for the next day.

Take charge of details: Take the time to create and maintain a computer folder that catalogs your job-search details: contact information, research ideas, thank-you notes, people to contact, sample resumes, etc. Organization will encourage a helpful sense of containment, not to mention save the time and energy you might have spent searching for scraps of information. Keep this external "brain" updated. As you input information, be sure to appreciate it for what it is: positive evidence of your efforts.

Brainstorm every day: Make this a slowlution. First, decide on the day's question or challenge. You might ask yourself something like, *How would my specific talents transfer into another field of work? ... What are all the ways I might connect with someone in X industry? ... What's helped me deal successfully with challenges in the past?*

To start your brainstorming session, place a pad and pen by your most comfortable chair. Settle in and close your eyes. Relax, breathing in and out peacefully, feeling the support of the chair beneath you, your feet on the floor. When you're at ease, invite your mind to open, calling in helpful images, sounds, or memories. Perhaps you invite "idea-clouds" to sail into your mind, or you imagine ideas washing up against you like a soft, warm summer tide.

Next, pose the day's question. Follow your thoughts the way a kite follows the wind. Dismiss none, judge none. When a thought strikes you as worth remembering, write it down; then, resume your brainstorming. Continue for 10-15 minutes. Keep your notes from day to day and see if you can identify helpful patterns and ideas.

Schedule slowlutions for certain times of day: Let their regularity form the backbone of days when you don't have appointments scheduled. If you're out and about, challenge yourself to contour your slow-downs to what you see around you: a park, or a comfortable armchair, perhaps. Slowlutions in which you connect with your body's rhythms, or with the grounding feel of the earth, can serve as reminders that your own structure is solidly intact.

Leave the house at least once each day: Give yourself a change of scenery, whether for networking, errands, or enjoyable pursuits. Remind yourself that the larger world exists and you're very much a part of it. Getting a part-time job, volunteering, or taking a class could provide wonderful ways to not only create structure, but also meet people who may help expand your job search.

Daniel did just that. He enrolled in real estate school. Although doing so didn't provide a long-term solution, it did provide structure for Daniel. "I'd get up in the morning, go to class, come home, do the work," he says. "I felt I had…something to do."

Revel in your enduring riches

No one wants to lose his or her source of income. Yet, there are many forms of riches left untouched by the loss of one's job. To counter the anxiety about money that's not coming in, call to mind all the non-financial bounty that is still present in your life.

The riches of your support system: Keep up your relationships with close family and friends. They will buffer you against isolation and stress. See yourself through their eyes: as someone whose gifts and qualities outshine your employment status. A slowing circle that focuses on the importance of regularly reducing stress and taking part in enjoyable pursuits can help buffer your job search activities.

The gift of choice: True, you're not in total charge of when you'll find your new job, but much personal choice remains. How you structure your job search may constitute your most powerful choice during this period. Consider your options carefully. Let your choice to regularly slow down serve as an empowering reminder of this gift.

The riches of relaxing and re-energizing: Your newly spare time arises from an unfortunate event; nonetheless, in between looking for work, take advantage of it: Write poetry, join a community club or walk in nature. For Nancy Rimes, going to the gym, as well as reading a favorite Bible quote - "Therefore, do not worry about tomorrow, for tomorrow will worry about itself" – made all the difference. Appreciate the rewards of these slower, richer experiences; no job can provide them – only you can.

Your enriching contributions: Use a slowlution to list your daily contributions to the life around you - despite being unemployed. Can a job hug your daughter, or help out your neighbors? Can it offer nuggets of wisdom, or drive your spouse to work? Even the most high-paying position can't pick up litter in the park or referee a soccer game. Notice your ongoing participation in life, and count yourself a fully contributing member.

The gift of free time: Your new free time is about far more than a lack of income. In fact, time is a currency you likely longed for when you were employed. Like a far-reaching vista, time offers you the space to reflect and gain perspective, as well as interact more frequently with friends and family. "It's been nice," says Nancy Rimes of her ability to offer more to her teen-aged son, "because [unemployment's] allowed me to be there when he needed it, because he's not going to need me that much longer." You have the choice to make this time one you'll remember as both challenging and rewarding.

Healthful benefits: If you've gained weight over the years due to stress and office candy jars, a newly open schedule can serve as an opportunity to improve your physical conditioning, as well as work off anxious energy. As with all slow-downs, start small and remember to practice kindness as you rework your exercise habits.

Optimizing your physical condition will feel empowering, imbuing you with greater confidence and energy for your job-search. Be grateful that your body works, that material wealth is not the only bounty in your life. Let awareness of your riches ground you when you become anxious about the future.

De-stress the topic of money (as much as you can)

"There's a little bird on one of my shoulders going 'You know that unemployment eventually runs out'," says Keith Spring. Keith's "bird" will likely pay you a visit. As a result, you may paint any downtime you take as negative. For Keith, time spent listening to music and reading could generate thoughts that he was "being lazy." Anxiety about money is entirely normal, but all too often it also brings on self-judgment; both, of course, contribute to tense activation and thinking about dire outcomes. To counter these, take the time to educate yourself about your financial reality.

Make a budget: In keeping with our stance of coexisting with anxiety, rather than avoiding it, sit down and go over your financial situation as soon as you emerge from the shock of losing your job (if you're single, ask someone skilled in finances or, at the least, a trusted friend to join you). This is not an easy task, but it's one that will ground you in reality; it bears repeating at regularly scheduled intervals.

Knowing that you've put all things financial on the table, have set a budget, and have a date review your finances again, will help you divert from ruminating about money. You'll more easily be able to tell yourself, *Today, I'm/we're fine. I have a plan and a budget and I'm following them. I have____ more weeks/months before I need to review things.*

Identify your financial safety net – before you need it: You'll recall that any experience of stress is related to the perception of how one's resources and demands match up. The more peaceful you feel about asking others for financial help, should you need it, the less stressed you will feel. Begin to lay the groundwork for this possibility before it becomes a necessity.

Of course, most people dread asking someone else for money. In our culture, we label the need for a personal loan as shameful. Yet, when matters such as shelter, food, and education are involved, how could such a request not be justified and honorable? Sit down with a trusted family member and friend and talk about the difference between monetary need and your identity and worth. To this end, it might prove helpful to recall that hardship is part of our human condition. Unemployment is currently the form your struggle has taken.

Before you talk with a prospective "safety net," slow down and mentally run through the interchange. Visualize the conversation several times; you might also want to role-play with someone. Don't fight your anxiety, and don't bolt from it; accept it, and then access your thinking. Prepare yourself to not take a "No" personally.

At the outset of the conversation, acknowledge how hard it is for you to ask. Review the efforts you've made to find work, as well as to budget (perhaps you're even working part-time). Emphasize that you know the prospective lender has his or her own pressures and may need to think about your request. They will want to know your plans for repaying a loan. If he or she does reply in the negative, be prepared to ask whether there's a possibility for some other type of assistance such being a reference for you, or providing you names for networking.

I encourage you to have this conversation long before you need it. It's unwise to assume a positive response for months, and then get a negative one when your bank account is that much slimmer. Tuck a Yes into a mental back-pocket; it will help you live with greater calm and that, in turn, will allow you to cultivate a balanced pace.

Creative finances: The recent economic downturn stimulated innovative financial tactics. Bargaining increased in retail establishments as customers sought breaks and stores sought sales. Before finalizing a transaction, you might want to do some bargaining. You could also offer services in lieu of payment. Initiate this suggestion by acknowledging its unusual nature, but explain that it's in keeping with your goal of managing your finances as creatively as possible.

Browse the web for do-it-yourself and "Maker Movement" communities in which people learn to provide their own services and create the things they previously bought. Tapping into these movements may save you money, expand your network, and provide you a stress-reducing sense of mastery.

Living in an anxious rush will not benefit your bank balance by even a penny. In fact, it may cost you money.

Consider the high cost of rushing

To encourage a slower, calmer approach to your job-search and to your life, remind yourself of the monetary costs of staying anxiously on the run. For instance, now is the time to recall that fatigue, distraction and haste are not only common ingredients of speedstress, they are also key factors in accidents and miscommunications.

Stress: Others in your household will be looking to you as a barometer for how stressed they "should" feel about the fact that you're unemployed. Not only that, everyone's mirror neurons will also be at work. Anxious rushing on your part will raise family members' stress, which will, in turn, raise yours.

Stress is costly in an emotional sense, of course, but it can also exact a financial price. For example, a foul, tense mood will seep into a job interview and losing one's temper with a creditor may ruin any chance for a new payment schedule. With greater calm, you'll be more purposeful in your interactions.

Now, can you expect yourself to be stress-free while unemployed? Of course not. But, purposefully cultivating a calm pace will help you *feel* calmer, sending an important signal to others.

Health: Stress lowers your ability to fight illness and it can raise your blood pressure, increasing your need for doctor visits. Fatigue can hinder thinking 'on your feet' in interviews, just as feeling rushed can cause you to speak unadvisedly, alienating others just when you need their support. Similarly, haste-induced falls or car accidents can result in expensive "repairs."

Relaxing, eating regularly and well, and getting adequate sleep and exercise, can help save you money.

Speed-accuracy trade-off: You'll find this applies to resumes and job applications. Don't set yourself up for missed job opportunities, not to mention wasted time and effort, by submitting documents with errors or missing information. Go slowly and get the details right when it counts.

What other financial savings can a calmer approach to job-hunting gain you?

Slow down for success in interviews

The chair of April Yvonne Garrett's former academic department once offered her advice about interviewing that she has long remembered: "You must be your most authentic self possible because the worst thing you can do is interview with a mask on. At some point ... *you* are going to show up."

Her advisor was right. It's very difficult to bluff your
way through an interview. The more prepared, balanced, and
grounded you feel, the more you'll impart that impression to your
interviewers. Consequently, before interviews, your first task is
to prepare in an unrushed manner; your second is to arrive at the
interview as balanced and rested as you can be.

Slow preparation

Speedstress is not your ally in interviews. Tense activation
will not help you smile in a genuine manner, think clearly, or
project a sense of calm reliability. In fact, research suggests that
fake smiles by interviewees result in less favorable impressions.
Job-seekers' evident anxiety during interviews can also lead to
more negative ratings.

Luckily, you can put slow's calming powers to work for you.
If you allow yourself enough preparation time before an interview, you will feel less stressed. So, as the date for an interview
draws near, re-gather your attention from less definite prospects.

Begin thinking of your interviewer as your ally. They are,
whether they hire you or not. A successful work situation is,
above all, about the match between the employee, his or her responsibilities, and the boss. If your prospective manager decides
they don't want you for the position, they'll be doing you a favor
by not hiring you. *Ally, ally, ally.* Maintain that internal stance
until you've walked out of their office door.

Research the company, field and the role you'd be filling.
Brainstorm how your skills, education, experience, character
attributes, and interests fit with the prospective position; prepare
to offer *specific* examples from your past experience. Ask your
friends for input; try to find someone at the company, or a similar

enterprise, to talk with. Build a case for your employment; envision yourself in the interview and on the job.

Equally important, *prepare* questions that demonstrate your knowledge of the field and enterprise in which you're interviewing. Have some questions on hand, as well, that explore the presence of attributes you'd like in your next workplace. The latter line of inquiry might investigate workload, expectations of employees, pacing, and supervisory support. You might want to ask about the interpersonal environment, any off-hours company traditions, or the company's philosophy about helping employees thrive.

Rehearse the interview in your mind. Picture yourself smiling as naturally as possible at appropriate moments. Once seated, you'll maintain a fairly straight posture, as well as meet your interviewer's eyes. Imagine how you'll handle an unexpected question, how you'll speak clearly in an unrushed, normal cadence. You may also want to talk yourself through the interview several times in an empowered manner: "I can and will walk into my ally's office with a real smile on my face ... I can and will ...".

In the last days before the interview, get enough rest and exercise so that you're as close to a state of calm energy as possible. Make sure you know where the meeting place is; leave enough time to get there without feeling rushed even *if* you hit traffic. If you arrive early, use a slowlution to help you relax: read a funny book, or take a walk, focusing on what you see and hear.

Just before you go into the interview, remind yourself that the interviewer got up and brushed their teeth this morning just like you did. If you were at a party, you would likely feel relaxed approaching him or her. Act as you would when meeting any new ally: Project warmth and confidence.

The job interview

Relationship-building begins from the moment we meet someone. First impressions in interviews, studies suggest, are important because they influence interviewers' evaluations. Make it your goal to transmit a sense of calm energy. Walk briskly into the room, look the interviewer in the eye, and shake hands with some firmness. Let the interviewer take the lead in positioning you in the office and opening the interview.

Put the focusing skills honed during *i slow* practice to work. Listen carefully and don't interrupt. Ask for clarification if you don't understand a question. Don't be afraid to take a moment to think before responding.

As your interviewer describes the position and the work culture, watch your interviewer's body language, and listen for moderate, rather than extreme, language. Try to assess how genuine they are.

As you leave, see if you can genuinely offer an appreciation for something you've learned, as well as for the opportunity to meet the interviewer. Always, email your thank-you in a timely fashion.

April took the advice she received in college to heart. When she went to an interview at a prestigious university, she allowed herself to wear a dress she felt good in – an orange one. She felt better – and it certainly made an impression. After she got the job, says April, her interviewer told her, "You were the only person who didn't show up with a boxy blue suit on."

After a turn-down

When you don't win a position, acknowledge your disappointment, but don't get lost in it. You will likely never know specifically why you didn't get hired, so divert from judgment. Instead, practice kindness by calling on reality. Rejection is part of the job-seeking process. Unless you acted patently crazy during your interview, a lack of an offer is usually based far less on *who* you are as a person (after all, how could they know *you*?), than it is on a wealth of other factors having to do with the fit between you and the job.

If you are sure you flubbed the interview, be willing to take the time to draw helpful lessons from the experience. A job search is exactly the time to recall the lesson that slowing down brings into sharp focus: Progress is possible, perfection isn't. Be glad that you know how to let yourself relax. Before you return to your job search, have some fun so that your mind can open to new possibilities. Then, move forward again.

For Keith Spring exercising a slower pace became integral to sustaining himself when he was unemployed. He spent time "catching up on reading that I like to do," he said, "and, again, listening to music without simultaneously doing some other chore or activity."

In the midst of stress, Keith created balance. I hope you will, too.

What's my slowlution?

⮎ What slowlution in this chapter seems most relevant to you? Put it into practice.

Chapter 22

An Open Field: Slowlutions for Parents and Children

"I said, 'Sophie, what's too structured?' and she said,
'I think the perfect summer camp would just be
an open field and your friends'."

~ Sharon Dornberg-Lee

The wisdom of children: When we set our sights on purposeful accomplishment, they remind us of the freedom and possibility to be found in an open field. As you listen for the answer to *What's my slowlution?*, don't overlook your children's wisdom, or their activities. Swinging, telling imaginary tales, or cheering madly at a school game offers wonderful distraction from stressors. When you're tense and tired, slowly and softly reading a calming bedtime story to your child, with full focus, can help both of you wind down.

Opening the field

To "open the field" for both your and your children's rest and revitalization, consider the possibility that their fun can be yours and your slow-downs can offer them gifts. You may want to try the following:

What's yours is mine: At times, you may want to involve your children very briefly in your slow-downs. Slowing down can teach young ones patience and relaxation techniques, as well as open them to new interests. As for their rest periods, try to make at least a portion of them yours as well. "It gives me permission to slow down. That's the time when … I put my feet up and rejuvenate myself," says Melany Coopmans.

Your care is theirs: When you are tired or sick and feel a need to cancel an outing with your child, give yourself a break: Remember that, even though your child may not recognize it, your well-being is more important to him or her than the outing is. Make *Caring for myself is caring for them* your motto; its truth is made evident by our knowledge about mirror neurons. Indeed, children's moods are often barometers of their parents'. "If [my husband and I] are stressed out, she'll be more in an angry place," notes Sharon Dornberg-Lee about her daughter.

So, keep your need for personal time in perspective, even if it means that your children experience some passing disappointment. Cancellations here and there won't cause their future to suffer. "It's ok to fail a little bit," notes Rebecca, the mother of twins, "because you're not failing …Your kid's not ruined because they've watched TV or because they had to eat a frozen pizza."

Slowlutions and Children: Encouraging a Natural Fit

Join children's fun, and make their downtime yours!

Enliven the everyday. Make simple tasks - dusting or setting the table, for example – fun for all of you.

Quiet Room: Introduce a brief quiet period each day for you and the kids (plus one before bed for them). In the "quiet room," nestle into a comfy spot. Lead the children in breathing slowly, drawing, stretching, or singing softly, etc. Then, let them make slowing down their own: Let them lead you …

Set boundaries: Boundaries, because of their protective and limiting nature, can help you rebalance when you're feeling overwhelmed. Saying *I'm going to take 2 minutes for quiet time* (set a timer if you have very small children) will model valuable skills that your children will carry into their adult lives.

... A Natural Fit

Behind my door: Introduce boundaries and self-care by framing in-your-room rest-time as so special that you want it, too. Take it! Afterwards, have a guessing game about what each did "behind my door." Share any resulting dreams, artwork, songs, etc.

Shape children's attention, and shape your own: Help your children to learn that their pace affects how they feel, see the world, and interact with others. Talk about your own pace.

If you feel guilty, remind yourself that not setting limits may mean that you're present physically, but not otherwise. "I think kids know when you're not present, when you're distracted," says Sharon. "[Sophie will] be like 'Mom, you're not paying attention' or 'You're always on the internet'."

Having set a boundary, you'll be more present when you do turn your attention back to your children, and they'll appreciate that.

s- and l-steps: Check in with your children about their tension and energy levels. Doing so will build their awareness, and yours. It will also help you head off stressful meltdowns. Ask yourself, *What's <u>their</u> slowlution?* Perhaps a play-date and a visit to the park are too much for them, as well as for you.

Ask your children: How do your children feel about their schedules and activity level? Don't assume you know! A 2006 *Kidshealth* survey of nearly nine hundred 9- to 13-year olds found that 90 percent reported feeling stressed because they were too busy! Sixty-one percent stated that they wanted much more free time to play and see friends. Sharon's eight year-old daughter Sophie gave her exactly that message while attending a summer music camp. "She was really complaining about it even though she loves to sing and dance ..." Sharon recalls. "She said 'I don't want to go from class to class'."

Value free time: Educators are belatedly realizing that cutting out recess is a bad idea: children learn better after being able to move and discharge their energy. Equal benefit is to be found in free time at home. Allowing your children the chance to amuse themselves will encourage self-sufficiency, as well as creativity. One of the most accomplished and mature teens I know was home-schooled – with a minimum of structure - until her high school years. I have no doubt that her self-assurance and creativity arises in part from having had the time to discover and pursue her interests and creative instincts. Help your children explore the spaciousness and treasure of free time – and let them see you doing the same.

Slowing Down with Teens at Home

Form a **slowing circle** with other parents. Help each other out with errands and driving; cheer each other's slowlutions.

In the pre-teen years, institute a **Calm Conversation Hour** once a week. Open each with a relaxation exercise that you each lead at differing times. Using ground rules that foster listening and calm, clear communication, talk about family successes and concerns.

Share one meal a day: Research points to a multitude of benefits (no technology or TV allowed).

Invite your teens to dream up **family outings**. Enjoy them for as long as they deign to attend!

Assign chores that both instill needed skills - for example, cooking, grocery-shopping, or child-care – and allow you to slow down.

Set clear limits with consequences that you can – and do! – enforce. This will benefit your teens, as well as save you all from stressful hours of arguing.

195

Your unhurried focus can transform even the most mundane aspects of parenting into "moon and tomato" moments. "If your overall goal is 'I want to be present to my children'," says Melany, whom we met under the moon with her daughter, "then changing diapers can be fun, but when you're trying to hurry to get to the next thing, you miss the enjoyment."

And so, we return to the garden where we first met. It's yours now to cultivate.

Conclusion

Chapter 23

Full Bloom:
The Rewards of Slowing Down

If we don't stop to listen, the bird's song is lost to us.

~ M.R. Place

A single day was all we had on the island of Capri.

As I rode the chairlift up to the isle's summit, bougainvillea, cypress, and lemon trees wove down into rocky outcroppings that edged aquamarine waters. The vista was captivating, yet it is not what I hold most dear when I think of that visit.

The day's greatest gift arose later, as a companion and I strolled down an alley that ran between the walls of gated courtyards. As we walked, admiring the stonework and flowers, I wondered about the homes behind the walls. Were they as charming as their surroundings suggested? What stories and traditions did they harbor? And then, I heard an aria, its high clear tones sparkling through the air. I slowed my pace, wondering where the singing came from.

I hesitated, and then walked back a few steps and crooked my head through an open gate into a garden courtyard. There, a radio perched on a table. A middle-aged man sat nearby on a chair. He rose, smiling as I tried to describe, with my few words of Italian, the beauty of the music.

The man must have understood, for he reached for one chair, then another. Setting them close to his, he gestured for my friend and me to sit down. The three of us were strangers for only an instant before the music's embrace drew us together. We listened as the opera singers' bright and full-throated voices filled the small courtyard. The opera originated, as our host managed to make clear, miles across the water in Naples. To me, its sound seemed imbued with the resonance of every opera ever sung across Italian time and history. In that short interlude, everything I'd ever hoped for from my trip converged: ease and welcome and a sense of being part of a land that was new to me.

As I look back, it's clear that in that moment of hesitation in the alley, I had a choice: To continue moving farther in our set direction, or to explore the tug I felt toward the notes rising through the air around us. It was not a difficult choice, not one in which anxiety prompted me toward one action or another. Yet, that sliver of hesitation held a possibility of loss identical to what occurs when, our attention firmly fixed on *Next!*, we repeatedly rush past our yearnings and needs. When we do that too often, our life's story loses dimension and resonance. We live, as the poet Rilke put it, "the life half-lived." Our onelife seems an unending plot line of tasks, tension and lack of control, our offerings to others far less than our balanced self would like.

When we slow down, we can choose to widen, taking in more of the world around us, and relating anew to our feelings, passions and talents. "Slowing down," says Geordie Robison, "has affected thinking about who I am, what I want to try, where I want to go in my life." After tiring of a life on the political campaign trail, of city lights obscuring night's bouquet of stars, Geordie moved to a small coastal town.

Happily, there's no need to wander from home base or to make big money in order to discover slow's powers.

Opportunities to rebalance from rushing to richness await only the breath of our awareness, intention and choice: The hug lingered in, rather than rushed by; curiosity followed, rather than ignored; nighttime tasks put aside for rest, reading, or intimacy. Wherever we are, so, too, are slowlutions.

Slowing down helped Marcy Litle weave a stronger relationship with her intuition. She lets her inner sense guide her more, rather than following what she refers to as "this template from the outside." Marcy has come to understand that attending to what's true for her in as many moments as possible also helps others. "I've discovered the more I can do that," she says, "the more present I am when I am out in the world, the smarter and kinder I can be in my dealings with other people."

The speed at which we choose to move, and the stress with which we do so, affects not only our loved ones and us, it also profoundly influences our communities. As illustration, I recall a Friday several years back when I was returning to my house, hurrying so as to get the car packed and leave town on time. I saw a neighbor who, 10 yards away in our local park, was clutching her ankle with one hand while holding on to several small, leashed dogs with her other. My reaction was quintessentially speed-stressed: "I have no time for this. I'm already late," I thought, and kept walking toward my home. Only when a neighbor hurried past me to help the woman did shame prompt me to do the same.

When we regularly live feeling that we have no time for ourselves, we offer a poverty of time and attention to others. Consequently, we unwittingly contribute to the alienation burgeoning in our world. "In order to have empathy for anyone else you have to have it for yourself," says Zelda Lockhart. "You have to know who you are and care about who you are and care about how you are connected to all other things."

When we are speedstressed, our lives can feel so degraded, our alienation from caring so complete that we don't see the human or environmental needs around us. Stressed, tired and anxious, it becomes all too easy for us to barrel by, quite unintentionally leaving bitter air in our wake. Only when we regularly offer ourselves kindness and balance can we send our innate generosity out into the world. The offering of our full attention, if only for a few moments, causes connection, healing, and meaning to bloom.

Similarly, when we slow down to attend carefully to what we're doing, the performance of even the most mundane tasks can provide rewards. "Regardless of what you have to do in your day," says Zelda Lockhart, "if you can find a way to find the grace and the gracefulness in every moment ... then you don't have to rush. Just be there and be in it."

Be there and be in it.

Zelda is talking about presence. That is exactly what Melany and Sylvia offered each other as they savored summer's warm red bounty in their moonlit garden. I hope that you, too, are well on the way to enjoying the richness of taking small moments to slow down and be present. Sarah is. At a "slower pace," she writes, "you really can smell the roses in people's gardens."

The roses have been there all along. It is we who must slow down to receive their gift and, having done so, pass it on.

Please see next page...

Composed Life Press
Durham, NC

Dear Reader,

Thank you so much for your interest in **Slowing Down in a Speedstressed World**. I sincerely hope that the book's been of assistance to you.

As an author who is self-publishing, I am – appropriately! - practicing slow-marketing. My marketing staff consists of myself – *and* as many enthusiastic and willing readers as possible. Consequently, getting the word out about this book depends on 3 resources only:

1. The book's quality
2. My marketing efforts
   &
3. The "people-power" of appreciative readers.

I hope that you're one of those readers, who will spread the word about slowing down and about this book.

If you benefitted from these pages, I will be so grateful if you do at least 1 of the following:

1. Tell others about the book; lend it or gift it.
2. Tweet about it/follow me at **@slowlutions**
3. "Like" the book & my website **www.slowlutions.com** on Facebook
4. Write a review on Amazon or other sites
5. Ask your local bookstore or your book club to order the book
6. Post the book's cover on Instagram or other sites
7. Email a review to me to post on my website **www.slowlutions.com**

You can easily share about the book through my website **www.slowlutions.com**.

Whatever you choose, please do it slowly and feel good about helping others to slow down. In fact, consider yourself a slowlution!

Thanks very much,

Marian

www.slowlutions.com

Notes

Introduction

Beneath the ever-changing ... each day.: ____. "Pennsylvania Station (New York City)." *Wikipedia*. Wikimedia Foundation, 29 June 2013. Web. [Note: Second dates noted in these citations refer to the last date on which the website information was viewed by author:] 4 July 2013. (Citedstatistic noted on Wikipedia website as from Jackson, Kenneth T., ed. Encyclopedia of New York City, pp. 498 and 891.)

Chapter 1

A 2012 American Psychological Association (APA) survey ... past five years: ____. "Stress in America: Our Health at Risk." *American Psychological Association* (APA), 2012, p. 15. Web. 4 July 2013.

Dave - and, perhaps, you ... lessen one's stress: Ibid., p. 20

After George W. Bush's ... lost perspective.": Urbina, Ian and Pear, Robert. "Former Aide's Arrest Surprises Friends and Colleagues." *New York Times*. 12 March 2006. Web. 4 July 2013.

The woman was ... to working.": Ludden, Jennifer. "College Grads Struggle to Gain Financial Footing." National Public Radio. 10 May 12. n. pag. Web. 4 July 2013.

Chapter 2

One factor which may ... insufficient sleep: ____. "Human Factors Analysis." *Report of the PRESIDENTIAL COMMISSION on the Space Shuttle Challenger Accident*. Vol. 2, Appendix G. n. pag. Presidential Commission on the Space Shuttle Challenger Accident, 1986. Web. 5 July 2013.

A 2012 American ... predominant stressors: "Stress in America: Our Health at Risk." *American Psychological Association*, p. 17.

203

A Gallup … personal satisfaction: Rheault, Magali. "3 in 10 Working Adults are Strapped for Time in the U.S." *Gallup/Wellbeing*. 20 June 2011. n. pag. Web. 5 July 2013 at http://www.businessinsider.com/in-us-3-in-10-working-adults-are-strapped-for-time-2011-7

One national poll … of spare time.: Carroll, Joseph. "Time Pressures, Stress Common for Americans: Nearly half do not have enough spare time, 40% are frequently stressed." *Gallup/Wellbeing*. 2 January 2008, p. 1. Web. 5 July 2013.

Typical effects of speedstress … practicing habitual behaviors.: King, Brian E. "How the Brain Forms New Habits: Why Willpower Is Not Enough." n.dat. Presentation Handout. Haddonfield, N.J.: Institute for Brain Potential, p. 11.
Chapter 3

In Thayer's book … of activation: Thayer, Robert E. *Calm Energy: how people regulate mood with food and exercise*. New York: Oxford University Press, 2001, p. 91.

Striking a pose … of testosterone.: Cuddy, Amy. *Your Body Language Shapes Who You Are*. TEDGlobal 2012 "TED Talk." Filmed June 2012. Web. 14 August 2013.

Chapter 5

…the brain's hypothalamus … hormone epinephrine.: McEwen, Bruce, et al. *The End of Stress as We Know It*. New York: Joseph Henry Press, 2002., pp. 23-24.

If cortisol remains … lowered immunity.: Ibid., pp. 61-62.

…when the sleep … blood-sugar regulation, appetite regulation…: Knutson, Kristen L. *Effect of Sleep and Sleep Loss on Glucose Homeostasis and Appetite Regulation*. Sleep Med Clin. 2007 June; 2(2): 187–197 [print]. Web. 20 September 2013.

Chapter 6

Patients who … 14 points: Nagourney, Eric. "The 5-Minute Guide for Lower Blood Pressure." *New York Times* 2 May 2006: D7. Print.

Naps, those most … 34 percent: Finney, Paul Burnham. "The Science of Zzzzz's." *The New York Times*. 8 August 2006. Web. 8 July 2013.

Wakeful breaks … to injury: "Take More Breaks to Avoid Back Injury at Work." *Newswise*. 8 February 2007. n. pag. Web. 6 July 2013.

Emotional positivity … skills: Fredrickson, Barbara L. *Positivity: Groundbreaking Research Reveals How to Embrace the Hidden Strength of Positive Emotions, Overcome Negativity, and Thrive*. New York: Random House, Inc., 2009. Print., p. 59.

Chapter 7

Specific types … with them: Iacoboni, Marco. *Mirroring People: The New Science of How We Connect with Others*. New York: Farrar, Straus and Giroux, 2008., pp. 4-5.

In fact, we … within seconds: Heathfield, Susan M. "Why "Blink" Matters: The Power of First Impressions. *About.com*. No date. n. pag. 6 July 2013. http://humanresources.about.com/ od/workrelationships/a/blink_effect.htm

Chapter 8

A recent study … were insufficient.: _____. "2013 Work and Well-Being Survey." *American Psychological Association* and *Harris Interactive*. March 2013. pdf pp. 3-18. Web. 8 July 2013.

"That" likely reflects … friendly service.: Galinsky, Ellen, et al. "Overwork in America: When the way we work becomes too much." *Families and Work Institute*, 2005, p.2. Web. 7 August 2013.

According to ComPsych … due to stress.: _____. "Presenteeism on the Rise as Employees Show Fatigue from a Slow- to No-Hire Economy." *ComPsych Corp.* 29 October 2012. n. pag. Web. 4 August 2013.

Employee morale … make it in to work.: _____. "The Hidden Cost of Absenteeism: New Workplace Options Absence Tracking Helps Businesses Mitigate Missed Work." n. pag. *Workplace Options*, 6 October 2010. Web. 9 July 2013.

In a 2007/ … from a job.: _____. "Playing to Win in a Global Economy: .2007/2008 Global Strategic Rewards Report and United States Findings." *Watson Wyatt Worldwide/World at Work*, 2008, p. 20. Web. 9 July 2013.

Turnover costs … employee's salary.: _____. "What are the Costs of Employee Turnover?" *AARP*. 14 April 2011, n. pag. Web. 3 May 2013.

In one experiment … make errors rises.: Chittka, L., et al. "Psychophysics: Bees Trade Off Foraging Speed for Accuracy." *Nature*, 24 July 2003, Vol. 424, p. 388. Web. 2 June 2012.

In a research- … target objects.: McCarley, Jason S. "Effects of Speed-Accuracy Instructions on Oculomotor Scanning and Target Recognition in a Simulated Baggage X-ray Screening Task" [Abstract]. *Ergonomics*, 2009, Vol 52, Issue 3, pp. 325-333. Web. 6 August 2013.

In 1925 … called Heligoland.: Cassidy, David C. *Beyond Uncertainty: Heisenberg, Quantum Physics, and the Bomb*. New York: Bellevue Literary Press, 2010.

The island's … interview years later.: Buckley, Paul and Peat, F. David (Interviewers) and Werner Heisenberg (Interviewee). "Werner Heisenberg 1901-1976," conducted early 1970s, n. pag. Web. http://www.fdavidpeat.com/interviews/heisenberg.htm. 23 February 2011.

A Harvard … $31 billion.: Dotinga, Randy. "Study Links Insomnia to $31.1 Billion in U.S. Workplace Errors." *HealthDay News*, 1 October 2012, n. pag. Web. http://health.usnews.com/health-news/news/articles/2012/10/01/study-links-insomnia-to-31-billion-in-us-workplace-errors. 6 August 2013.

At Apple … from those visits.: Isaacson, Walter. *Steve Jobs*. New York: Simon & Schuster, 2011.

According to ComPsych … day of productivity…: ____. "Presenteeism on the Rise as Employees Show Fatigue from a Slow- to No-Hire Economy." *ComPsych Corp.* 29 October 2012. n. pag. Web. 7 August 2013.

…while a 2009 survey … affected their output.: ____. "Stress in America 2009." *American Psychological Association* (APA), 2009, p. 16. Web. 7 August 2013.

Chapter 9

"Everything rests … of motivation.": Claudia Horwitz. *Interview with author.* 10 November 2006. Durham, N.C. Ms. Horwitz was repeating the words of her meditation teacher, Joseph Goldstein.

... a rocky wave-pounded ... as "blue hell.": Zuma, Jacob. "Address by the Deputy President, Jacob Zuma, at the Official Opening of the University of Western Cape (UWC)-Robben Island Mayibuye Archives," 13 June 2001. <http://www.info.gov.za/speeches/2001/0106141045a1001.htm> 6 July 2013.

Mr. Mandela and other ... it with soil.: Mandela, Nelson. "Spirit of Freedom: Drawings & Narratives from Nelson Mandela's Imprisonment at Robben Island." Viewed 30 September 2007. Durham County Public Library, Durham, NC.

Recounting the loss ... loving relationships.: Mandela, Ibid.

Chapter 11

Research has found ... more competitive: Carey, Benedict. "Who's Minding the Mind?: The Subconscious Brain is More Active,Independent and Purposeful than Once Thought. Sometimes It Takes Charge." *The New York Times.* 31 July 2007. Pp. D1, D6. Print.

Social connectedness ... to stress...: Wait, Marianne, Ed. *Looking After Your Body: An Owner's Guide to Successful Aging.* Pleasantville, N.Y.: Readers Digest Association, 2001, p. 198. Print.

...positive feedback ... changing habitual behaviors: Trafton, Jodie A., Gordon, William P., and Misra, Supriya. *Training Your Brain to Adopt Healthful Habits: Mastering the Five Brain Challenges.* Los Altos, CA: Institute for Brain Potential, 2011., pp. 171-2. Print.

Gatherings invite ... increase circulation.: Pink, Daniel. *A Whole New Mind: Moving from the Information Age to the Conceptual Age.* New York: Riverhead Books, 2005., pp. 193, 5.

Early on in ... act on your intention.: Trafton, et al., pp.174-176.

Chapter 13

Keep in mind ... six months: Trafton, et al., p. 171.

Chapter 15

Psychologist Lera Boroditsky ... perceptions and thoughts.: Begley, Sharon. "What's in a Word? Language May Shape Our Thoughts." *Newsweek.* 9 July 2009. Web. 29 March 2011.

In fact, according … less than one second.: Author notes of presentation by David Burns, M.D. at workshop: "Scared Stiff: Fast, Effective Treatment for Anxiety Disorders." Workshop organized by the *Institute for the Advancement of Human Behavior*. Held in Durham, North Carolina: 30-31 March 2007.

Chapter 17

Positive emotions … forming it).: Fredrickson, p. 57, 59.

Because of this … do negative ones.: Fredrickson, p. 32.

When making decisions … piece of paper.: Malkin, Elisabeth. "New Commitment to Charity by Mexican Phone Tycoon." *The New York Times*. 28 June 2007. n. pag. Web. 22 September 2013.

Chapter 19

When our food … of physiological stress.: King, p. 11 and personal notes.

According to a … likely to quit.: _____. "Gallup Study: Engaged Employees Inspire Company Innovation." *Gallup Business Journal*, 12 October 2006. n. pag. Web. 21 September 2013.

Chapter 20

The British author … early 20th century.: Sitwell, George. *On the Making of Gardens*. Boston: David R. Godine, publisher, 2003.

Chapter 21

In fact, research … favorable impressions.: Dean, Jeremy. "10 Psychological Techniques to Help You Get a New Job." PSYBLOG. 24 August 2011. n. pag. Web. 21 September 2013.

Job-seekers' evident … more negative ratings.: McCarthy, Julie and Goffin, Richard. "Measuring Job Interview Anxiety: Beyond Weak Knees and Sweaty Palms." *Personnel Psychology*, Autumn 2004, Vol. 57, Issue 3. n. pag. Web. 21 September 2013.

You may also … empowered manner…: Dean, Jeremy.

Made in the USA
San Bernardino, CA
25 March 2014